PRAISE FOR
DIFFERENCE MAKER

"*The Difference Maker Series* is pure genius. We've all been wounded, and this book offers concrete, specific things that readers can do to help with the healing process. It's clear that the author cares deeply for and is passionate about assisting others to find a new life of powerful, positive impact."

—Dr. Craig Borchardt, CEO Hospice Brazos Valley, Texas A&M Health Science Center

"*Difference Maker* is an impactful and practical guide for wounded souls. Changed thinking is a first step toward changed behavior. Gary masterfully connects heart and head matters in this book. I look forward to sharing it with clients and friends."

—Carrie Andree, Licensed Professional Counselor

"*Difference Maker* is a must read for anyone contemplating self-harm, struggling with depression, or knows somebody who is. We – each of us – can make a huge difference in the world, and this book can help."

—Dr. Doug Vance, PhD, Juvenile Justice & Corrections Consulting

"No one is beyond repair. Anyone can heal. Everyone can make a difference. These are the messages we all need to hear. Gary has done a marvelous job of addressing what holds us back and what can propel us forward. We must embrace who we are and who we can be, and not merely who we've been."

—Paul Casale, Licensed Mental Health Counselor, Marriage & Family Therapist

"We can find ourselves lost without purpose or direction. Many end up in a hopeless downward spiral. Gary's insight in getting to the heart of the issue and focusing on the real battle, which is the battle for the mind, brings hope and clarity instead of hopelessness and confusion. I will definitely recommend this book."

—Page Bratcher, Divorce & Life Recovery Coach

DIFFERENCE MAKER

OVERCOMING ADVERSITY AND TURNING PAIN INTO PURPOSE, EVERY DAY

GARY ROE

Difference Maker

Copyright © 2019 by Gary Roe All rights reserved.
First Edition: 2019

ISBN: 978-1-950382-11-8

Cover and Formatting: Streetlight Graphics

No part of this book may be reproduced, scanned, or distributed in any printed or electronic form without permission. Please do not participate in or encourage piracy of copyrighted materials in violation of the author's rights. Thank you for respecting the hard work of this author.

The author is not engaged in rendering medical or psychological services, and this book is not intended as a guide to diagnose or treat medical or psychological problems. If you require medical, psychological, or other expert assistance, please seek the services of your own physician or licensed professional counselor.

OTHER BOOKS BY GARY ROE

Living on the Edge: How to Fight and Win the Battle for Your Mind and Heart

Difference Maker: Overcoming Adversity and Turning Pain into Purpose, Every Day (Teen Edition)

Comfort for Grieving Hearts: Hope and Encouragement for Times of Loss
(Winner, 2018 Best Book Awards)

Teen Grief: Caring for the Grieving Teenage Hearts
(Winner, 2018 Book Excellence Award)

Shattered: Surviving the Loss of a Child
(2017 Best Book Awards Finalist)

Please Be Patient, I'm Grieving
(2016 Best Book Awards Finalist)

Heartbroken: Healing from the Loss of a Spouse
(2015 Best Book Awards Finalist, National Indie Excellence Award Finalist)

Not Quite Healed
(Co-Authored with Cecil Murphey)

Saying Goodbye: Facing the Loss of a Loved One

Welcome.
Don't read this book just once.
Come back to it in three months, six
months, or a year. Read it again.
You'll be surprised, and encouraged by your progress.
You'll be stunned by the Difference Maker you've become.

To help you with this process, I've prepared
a free download for you.

Difference Maker Summary and Goal Setting Helps

https://www.garyroe.com/difference-maker-goal-setting

DEDICATION

This book is dedicated to my early mentors:
Ronnie Rogers, Tom Harrison, and Lendol Calder.

You dared to believe I was a Difference Maker.
Thank you.

ACKNOWLEDGEMENTS

Special thanks to my lovely wife Jen, for her unwavering support and encouragement. You play such a massive role in all I do and in everything I write. You are a blessing beyond description.

Special thanks to Kathy Trim, Anni Welbourne, and Kelli Reynolds for their editing prowess and continual support, project after project. Your attention to detail makes such a huge difference.

Thanks to Dr. Craig Borchardt, CEO of Hospice Brazos Valley, for his continual support of my writing. Thank you for keeping me focused on the bigger picture and helping me think outside the box.

Thanks to Glendon Haddix and Streetlight Graphics for bringing this manuscript to life with superb artwork and formatting. You make us all look good.

Thank you, Difference Makers. I'm honored to know you.

THE DIFFERENCE MAKER GPS
(Where We're Going)

Part One: Gearing Up for Battle

Part Two: Exposing the Bad Stuff
(Rejecting the Lies That Hold You Back)

Part Three: Embracing the Good Stuff
(Believing the Truths That Propel You Forward)

Part Four: Hurdling Obstacles
(Conquering Things That Trip You Up)

Part Five: Mission Launch!
(Discovering Why You're Here and Living Your Purpose)

TABLE OF CONTENTS

DEDICATION 5

ACKNOWLEDGEMENTS 7

THE DIFFERENCE MAKER GPS
(Where We're Going) 9

WHAT THIS BOOK IS ALL ABOUT
(What You'll Get Out of This, If You're Willing) 15

PART ONE: GEARING UP FOR BATTLE 17
    Chapter One FIGHT! 19
    Chapter Two A TALE OF BATTLE 23

PART TWO: EXPOSING THE BAD STUFF
(Rejecting the Lies That Hold You Back) 31
    Chapter Three LIES, LIES, AND MORE LIES 33
    Chapter Four I'M UNLOVABLE 35
    Chapter Five I'M WORTHLESS 37
    Chapter Six I'M NOT ENOUGH 39
    Chapter Seven I'M ALONE 41
    Chapter Eight I'M DAMAGED 43
    Chapter Nine I'M INVISIBLE 45
    Chapter Ten I'M UGLY 47
    Chapter Eleven "IT'S ALL SOMEONE
    ELSE'S FAULT" 49

PART THREE: EMBRACING THE GOOD STUFF
(Believing Truths that Propel You Forward) 55

Chapter 12 I'M VALUABLE 57

Chapter 13 I'M NOT PERFECT 61

Chapter 14 IT'S NOT ABOUT
MY APPEARANCE 65

Chapter 15 I CAN HEAL 69

Chapter 16 I'M SIGNIFICANT 73

Chapter 17 I'M LOVABLE 79

Chapter 18 I'M FAR FROM ALONE 85

PART FOUR: HURDLING THE OBSTACLES
(Conquering Things That Can Trip You Up) 97

   Chapter 19 BIG DEATHS, LITTLE
DEATHS, AND OTHER BAD STUFF 99

   Chapter 20 ANGER 105

   Chapter 21 FEAR AND ANXIETY 111

   Chapter 22 SADNESS, DEPRESSION,
AND SUICIDAL THOUGHTS 117

PART FIVE: LAUNCHING YOU ON YOUR MISSION!
(Discovering Why You're
Here and How to Live Your Purpose) 127

   Chapter 23 MISSION CRISIS! 129

   Chapter 24 MISSION DEFINED 133

   Chapter 25 MISSION BUSTERS 143

   Chapter 26 MISSION BUILDERS 153

   Chapter 27 MISSION LAUNCH! 167

   Chapter 28 WHERE DO YOU
GO FROM HERE? 171

   Chapter 29 PUTTING IT ALL TOGETHER 177

Chapter 30 MY AMAZING
DIFFERENCE-MAKING MENTOR ... 181

RESOURCES FOR DIFFERENCE MAKERS ... 185

FREE ON GARY'S WEBSITE ... 187

ABOUT THE AUTHOR ... 189

AN URGENT REQUEST ... 191

WHAT THIS BOOK IS ALL ABOUT
(What You'll Get Out of This, If You're Willing)

I WAS 16 YEARS OLD.
    I had been hit too many times. I was stunned, frustrated, and confused. I was depressed, but I didn't know what that was.

Life had become harsh. Painful. Confusing. I began wondering if life was worth it.

I engaged in risky behavior. Things were going downhill. Then I caught a break. A big one.

I woke up.

I realized the world was broken. The brokenness seemed to be everywhere and in everything.

I realized that people were broken. All of them. Even the ones who looked like they had it all together.

I realized I was broken.

Then I got angry.

I decided to act. I might be broken, but I wasn't going to be a doormat for depression, anxiety, or fear.

I decided to become a Difference Maker.

I didn't know I was making this decision at that time. I just wanted things to be different. I believed things *could* be different.

So, I started doing things differently.

I decided to take the pain and adversity I encountered and turn it into something good, somehow, some way.

That saved my life.

I've grown, and I'm still growing. I've healed, and I'm still healing. Difference-making isn't easy, but it's always good.

WHAT YOU'LL GET OUT OF THIS BOOK

Here are some of the things you'll get out of this book, if you're willing:

- You'll learn a lot about yourself.
- You'll discover that much of what you struggle with has to do with lies you've been fed and bought into along the way. We'll expose those lies.
- You'll learn what's really true about you and what to do with that.
- You'll learn how to overcome obstacles that threaten to trip you up or even take you out.
- You'll discover how absolutely crucial and critical it is to discover and define your mission. We'll do that together.
- You'll learn why you're here and what to do with that.
- By the end of this book, you'll hopefully be able to look in the mirror and say, *"I'm a Difference Maker."* And when you really believe that, you'll begin to live it out.

Difference-making is a journey. It doesn't happen with the click of a mouse. You don't get there overnight. There is no magic pill for this. But you can start making a difference today.

Yes, today. Immediately.

Are you game?

I hope so. The world needs you.

PART ONE:
GEARING UP FOR BATTLE

Prepare for battle.
The world is tough. Life can be brutal.
You've been hit and wounded.
You don't have to let what happened control your life.
Stand up. Take a deep breath.
Prepare to fight.

CHAPTER ONE
FIGHT!

I'M INVITING YOU — ASKING you — to fight.

Fight for yourself. Fight for those you care about. Fight for all those around you. Fight to make a difference in a broken and hurting world that desperately needs you.

Yes, you.

You can make far more of a difference than you realize.

Difference-making has little to do with, in my opinion, how much money you have, what kind of place you live in, how talented you are, or your level of education.

Difference-making is about your heart. We all have one of those. Anyone can be a Difference Maker, anytime, anywhere.

You might feel depressed, anxious, worthless, and deeply wounded. That might be how you feel *now*, but now is not the future. One of the greatest lies we can believe is, *"It will always be this way."*

The companion lie that follows it is even more devastating: *"I will always be this way."*

Lies.

Now is not forever. Things will change. You can change. You can heal and grow.

Again, I'm asking you to fight. You're worth it. So are those around you.

WHAT'S THIS BATTLE ALL ABOUT?

This battle — the right to become the Difference Maker you were designed to be — is all-important. It is a fight for your heart.

We'll talk more about this later. For now, I'll just say this...

Your heart is your most prized possession. All of your life comes from it, one way or another. What you do with your heart is the most important thing about you.

Your heart wants to be significant and to make a difference. Deep down, you know you were made for impact. You long for purpose and meaning.

This battle is about finding and unearthing your heart.

Maybe your heart has been buried. Perhaps it's suffocating. It gets pounded every day with powerful messages, traumatic images, and an overwhelming amount of information. The world spins quickly. Life moves with blazing speed. You get hit, hurt, and wounded. The world drags on, and pulls you along with it.

You've been hyperventilating inside without even knowing it. You're nervous. Anxious. Scared.

Inside, way down deep, your heart is screaming.

Your heart is in danger.

If you don't act, the world and the hits of life will likely silence it. You can't afford to let that happen.

You must find your heart. You must dig it out from amid all the debris it's buried under.

You must free your heart. When you do, difference-making will become automatic.

Freeing the heart, however, isn't easy, quick, or simple. At first, it's easy to confuse the world's voice with your own. You've gotten used taking in messages from the outside. If these messages are powerful and frequent enough, you can begin believing them. You begin to hear messages that did not come from you in your own voice.

This is the gutsiest part of the fight. The battlefield is your mind.

You must become aware of and expose the lies you've been living. We'll do that together.

Then you must discover the truth about yourself and those around you. We'll do that together too.

Then you must believe and begin to live out who you really are, from your heart. We'll talk about how to do that.

As you do these things, you'll find yourself living more and more from your heart. You'll become more of who you were designed and destined to be.

You'll be a Difference Maker.

THE BATTLE IS ON. LET THE JOURNEY BEGIN.

This is a journey. It's a fight.

It's not easy. It might even get unbelievably hard at times.

Fight on. Stay the course. Your heart is worth it.

Fight against living a small and shrinking life.

Fight against going through the motions and living on auto-pilot.

Fight against hiding and living according to everyone else's expectations.

Fight against letting your heart be overly influenced by what others have done or said.

Fight against letting your mind be controlled by what has happened to you or around you.

Fight for yourself. Fight for those you love and care about.

Fight for your heart.

You'll be glad you did. So will everyone else around you.

Let's get going. The world needs you.

> *Difference Makers sense there is a battle raging. Their minds and hearts are under assault. Rather than run, they begin to train themselves for this fight.*

CHAPTER TWO
A TALE OF BATTLE

You deserve to know who's talking to you.

My name is Gary. I grew up in a small family. I have one brother, who is 14 years older. Dad owned and ran an auto salvage business. Mom worked as a nurse. I thought of us as an average middle-class family. Things looked pretty good on the outside, but inside was another story.

My parents' marriage wasn't good. Raised voices were part of the daily routine. Screaming was common. If Mom and Dad weren't at each other's throats, they were punishing each other with cold, silent anger.

Mom was slowly slipping into mental illness, but none of us knew that. It got worse as time went on. She remained functional at work, but at home she was demanding, irrational, and delusional. Dad didn't know what to do. Depression set in. Seeking help for such things was still taboo.

In addition to this, I lost large chunks of my childhood to sexual abuse. It continued over several years. There were several perpetrators. This skewed everything for me — how I saw life, people, and myself. I tried to become invisible. If I made myself as small as possible, perhaps I could go unnoticed and escape more abuse, anger, and disappointment. When I started school, I was embarrassed about me. I hid. I went internal and hardly ever talked to anyone. I felt different — damaged.

I lost both grandfathers so early that I never really knew them.

One grandmother never knew who I was because of dementia. My dad's family was warm and welcoming, but Mom managed to separate us from them. My brother was away at college and then on to his career. For all practical purposes, *family* meant the three of us — me, Mom, and Dad. Life was not fun.

Here are some messages I believed growing up.
"I'm damaged goods."
"I'll never be good enough."
"I'm small."
"I'll never be a real man."
"I'm worthless."
"No one will ever love me."

Trying to be invisible wasn't working, so I became a performing animal. I reasoned, *"If I perform well enough, maybe I can get some of what I need from others."* I didn't know it, but I was looking for love and acceptance.

I became an overachieving robot. In school, I made nothing but A's. If I wasn't the best, the kid with the highest score on every test in each subject, I was a failure.

I was also small. Small and smart was not a good combo for endearing me to my classmates. I was taunted, laughed at, shoved around, and bullied almost every day.

I learned to swim, and I was good at it. I joined a team and spent hours each day in the pool. I outperformed my small stature and was nationally ranked by the time I was 10.

The awards and accolades came. I enjoyed them for a few days, and then jumped back on the performance treadmill. I was compelled. Driven. I didn't know it, but I was being pushed along by shadows.

In seventh grade, a good friend of mine named Jeff died suddenly of an illness over Christmas break. He was bright, funny, and full of promise. We got along well. I felt accepted by him. We understood each other. He sat directly in front of me in homeroom.

I spent the rest of the year starting each day staring at his empty desk.

I remember asking myself, "Why?"

That was the first time I remember asking that three-letter question. Once I asked it about Jeff, I began asking "Why?" about the rest of life too.

Soon after Jeff's death, my parents separated and then divorced. By default, I lived with Mom. She slipped further into mental illness to the point where she was no longer functional. She was admitted to the local psychiatric hospital. I moved in with Dad.

The time with Dad was the best 6 months of my life up to that point. He was stable and beginning to take care of himself. I adored our simple man cave, which I dubbed, "The Bachelor Pad." My friends loved him. He even went with us to a Queen concert. I was beginning to feel safe.

Then one Sunday afternoon, Dad collapsed on the kitchen floor while cooking lunch. I heard the pots and pans fall. I ran in, saw him gasp, and then stop breathing. They managed to resuscitate his heart at the hospital, but too much time had gone by. He never regained consciousness. No brain activity. After a week on life support, my brother and I nodded our heads and gave permission for the machines to be turned off. Dad died a few hours later.

My world, as I knew it, was over. I was 15.

I put on a good act. I kept performing as usual, both academically and athletically. I sent the message loud and clear — *"No blips here. I'm fine. I've got this. No problem."*

Mom, who was now out of the hospital, moved in. She was more unstable than before. One night, she attempted to take her own life. The EMT's resuscitated her and loaded her on the cart.

One said to me, "Are you coming to the hospital with us?"

I shook my head no.

I went back to bed, angry and numb. I remember saying to myself, *"Whatever."*

The next morning, I got up, went to swim practice and then school like nothing had happened. Mom was put in psychiatric care again, and I lived alone for several weeks. I guess I flew under everyone's radar, unnoticed.

Maybe I was invisible after all.

I thought, *"If this is what life is, I'm not sure I'm going to make it. I'm not sure I want to make it."*

Just before Mom was released from the hospital, a good friend from swim team and his dad showed up at my door. They invited me to come live with them, with Mom's permission. I had known this family for almost 10 years and had been in their home numerous times. To my surprise, Mom said yes.

I packed up my stuff and Mom and I headed over to their house. When they answered the door, Mom said, "Here's Gary. I'm going to Vegas." She smiled, turned around, walked back to the car, and drove off. I didn't see her for several years.

I remember standing there, not at all surprised by this display. I was used to it. I suddenly realized that, for all practical purposes, I was an orphan.

"Whatever," I said to myself again.

I looked up at my new family family standing in the doorway. I felt embarrassed, ashamed, and incredibly small.

They stepped out, hugged me, picked up my stuff, and in we went.

Life was never the same after that. I didn't know it, but my journey of healing had begun.

I was excited, but I felt weird too. They were so different from what I was used to. I was raised as basically an only child and now found myself in a household of seven. It was wild, busy, active, and incredibly stable.

I thought I knew what stable was. Turns out I didn't have a clue. My heart was cautious. I didn't dare trust too soon. I had been disappointed and wounded too many times. I was hesitant. I held back.

The love and acceptance of this family was so powerful, however, that I finally let down my guard. I began to feel safe. Really safe. And that felt so very good. It's like I started breathing for the first time. Maybe I had been holding my breath my whole life. Being surrounded by health, love, and encouragement was a shock.

Frankly, it was wonderful.

My heart began to settle. A resolve surfaced deep inside me. Far from giving in or giving up, I wanted to fight — fight for myself and my healing.

I knew that life was tough and full of unwanted shocks and surprises. I was determined to learn to handle the hits well and find ways to use them for good.

My last two years of high school, I launched out on a mission to heal and grow. I was ready to turn all the pain around and make a difference somehow. I discovered that the best revenge against the past is not letting it determine the future.

I studied Psychology in college and then headed to Seminary. From there I served as a college minister, a missionary to Japan, and a pastor. I now currently work as an author, speaker, hospice chaplain, and grief counselor. My adult life has been focused on healing and growing from the hits of life, and then helping others do the same.

We've all been wounded. I know you have too. That's why you're reading this.

You might be saying, *"Whatever,"* right now. I get that.

You might be feeling small, even invisible. Maybe you feel worthless, damaged, or ugly. Perhaps you feel *"not enough."* I get that too.

I'm here to tell you that you matter — more than you know. I'm hoping that this book will make a difference in your life — a big one.

Here's the bottom line. Bad things happen – even evil things. You can let what happens control you and steal your life, or you can do something different.

You can *be* different.

You can take whatever has happened and choose to use it for good.

You can choose to heal and grow.

Read on.

> ***Difference Makers know that bad things happen.***
> ***Instead of giving in, they become committed to finding***
> ***ways to turn loss and pain into something good.***

We know that a battle is raging.
Our minds and hearts are under assault.
Bad things happen to us and to those we care about.
Fear, anxiety, and uncertainty are everywhere.
Rather than turning cynical or giving in, Difference Makers begin training themselves for this fight – the battle of using loss, tragedy, and pain for good.
We are Difference Makers.

PART TWO:
EXPOSING THE BAD STUFF
(Rejecting the Lies That Hold You Back)

IT'S TIME WE EXPOSED THE bad stuff.

You know it's there. Deep down. Lurking.

You're human. You're less than perfect, and so is everyone around you. You grew up surrounded by imperfection.

You got hurt. You were disappointed. You experienced loss. You tried to make sense of these things. You were impacted by the messages that surrounded you.

Negative messages have extraordinary power. They get our attention. They smack the heart and wriggle their way in. Lies are planted, take, root, and begin to grow.

These lies become part of the grid through which you see and interpret life and relationships. These untruths weave themselves into your personal prescription lenses, significantly influencing the clarity of your vision.

These lies can suck your heart dry. They can steal your life.

You can't let that happen. You're too important.

You might doubt the truth of the previous sentence. Of course. The lies have colored your perception.

It's time to unmask these culprits.

CHAPTER THREE
LIES, LIES, AND MORE LIES

Lies.

We all have them, somewhere deep inside us.

They could be messages that were given to us. Perhaps we heard them from others around us through words, body language, actions, or absence. They could even be things that we made up, internalized, and now act on.

You get bombarded with messages every day. Not all of them are true. Some are true, but not helpful. Others might even be mean and cruel.

Your heart senses these messages. They swirl around you, seeking a way in. All of them effect you, but you get to decide which ones linger in your mind and slip into your heart. Ultimately, you choose what you're going to believe.

When you were younger, however, you naturally believed the words and actions of those around you — especially family and others you spent a lot of time with. These messages shaped your mind and heart. They influenced you profoundly.

Though these messages came from others, over time you got so used to them that you began hearing them in your own voice. You began telling yourself, *"I'm this...I'm that."*

What are some of the more common lies we believe? They usually include some version of the following words:

Unlovable.

Worthless.

Damaged.
Failure.
Hopeless.
Not good enough.
Alone.

These words, and the ideas that come from them, spear the heart. They penetrate to the core of our being. Like little viruses injected one message at a time, they can wreak havoc in every area of life.

These words form the foundation from which lies are constructed. If the foundation is flawed, everything you build on top of it will be affected. You need to make sure what you're constructing – your life – is on solid, level ground.

It's time for a foundation inspection. Time to unearth the lies, the enemies of your heart.

> **Difference Makers are on guard against the**
> **lies that have infiltrated their hearts.**
> **To the foes of our hearts:**
> **Look out. We're coming for you.**

CHAPTER FOUR
I'M UNLOVABLE

"*I'M UNLOVABLE.*"
This lie comes in a variety of forms.
"*No one will ever really love me.*"
"*I'm ugly.*"
"*I'll never measure up.*"
"*I'm hopeless.*"

WE LOOK FOR LOVE.

Love. We come out of the womb looking for it. We need it desperately. It's oxygen to our souls.

We search for it. We look for it in the faces of those around us. We hunger and thirst for it. We can't survive without it.

Love.

What is it anyway?

Some view it as a feeling.

That would be nice, but it's far more than that. If love is merely an emotion, it comes and goes. If love is a feeling, you begin to live at the whim of your emotions. Mood becomes king.

Moods are something to pay attention to but are not a foundation to build your life on. They are like shifting sand. Here one moment and gone the next.

Your heart needs more certainty than this. You need love.

By its nature, love is unconditional. Love accepts you where you are, as you are. Love enters your world and meets you there.

Love accepts you where you are but doesn't leave you there. Love moves you toward healing and growth. Love nurtures and encourages you to become the best you possible.

Love is indispensable. Essential. Absolutely necessary. Long term, no heart can survive without it.

"I'm unlovable," is a lie. The following, however, could be truths:

"I don't feel loved right now."

"I don't feel accepted."

"I don't feel heard or seen."

"I feel rejected."

The operative word in the above statements is *feel*.

Here is the truth: Everyone is lovable. The trouble is that life is tough. Your heart gets hit. Others' hearts get hit too. We tend to take out our pain on each other. None of us is perfect. We get hurt, and we hurt others.

If a heart gets wounded enough, it goes into hiding. We conclude, *"Life is a farce. I'm a loser. No one will ever really love me."*

We sigh. Our hearts whisper, *"I'm unlovable."*

That's a lie. You might *feel* unlovable — maybe a lot. This disconnect between what feels true and what is true reveals a profound truth about emotions: Feelings are real, but they are not necessarily reality.

In other words, you can feel like no one loves you, when the reality is that many people do.

Again, feelings are real, but they are not necessarily reality.

More on this later.

On to the next common lie...

CHAPTER FIVE
I'M WORTHLESS

"*I'M WORTHLESS.*"
This lie comes in several other forms as well.
"*I'll never amount to anything.*"
"*I'm bad.*"
"*I'm a mistake.*"
"*I'm no good to anyone.*"
"*I'm a loser.*"

Are there times when we feel worthless? Yes. Does this make it true? No.

IMPERFECT IS A LONG WAY FROM WORTHLESS.

We all fail. A lot. All the time.

Our problem is we look around and see people we think have it all together. I mean, they look like they have it altogether, so surely, they do, right?

Wrong.

No one has it together. Everyone, on some level, is wearing a mask. We're all protecting ourselves, or trying to -- some more than others. None of us is fully ourselves all the time. No one person is anywhere close to being perfect.

We're all imperfect. You're imperfect. Yet, imperfect is a far cry from worthless.

Worthless means to be without meaning. No purpose. Good for nothing.

Our personal brands of perfectionism are taking a toll on us.

Perfectionism will kill your heart. It won't help your relationships either. Dump it now. Accept the truth that you're imperfect and wounded. No one has it together. We're all trying to find our way.

And we're all in this together.

That's part of our purpose and meaning. We are meant walk together through these challenges. We're designed for relationship and wired for connection. We need each other, badly.

You might feel worthless or like a mistake. *"I feel worthless,"* might be true. *"I'm worthless,"* is a blanket statement about you all the time, everywhere.

"I'm worthless," is a lie.

You're more valuable than you know.

We'll talk more about this later too.

On to another lie many of us believe....

CHAPTER SIX
I'M NOT ENOUGH

"*I*'M NOT _____ *ENOUGH.*" You fill in the blank.

Not good enough. Not smart enough. Not big enough. Not pretty enough, talented enough, or rich enough. Not successful enough, young enough, or healthy enough.

Not enough.

Almost everyone I have ever met feels this way. Yes, even those who are arrogant and spend all their time showing us they have it together. Deep inside of all of us there is this voice, sometimes shouting, sometimes whispering, *"Not enough."*

TRYING TO BECOME *ENOUGH.*

What do we do with this?

Most of us try to prove ourselves somehow. We try to become *enough*.

We figure out what others want and give it to them. We become chameleons constantly changing color to better fit into the current group or situation. We compare, and compare, and compare.

And when we compare, we lose. There will always be someone better, more talented, more successful, more attractive, or more intelligent.

No wonder we feel *not enough*.

"Not enough," is a lie.

This lie is based on comparison between imperfect, fallible

human beings in an imperfect and fallible world. We're all wounded, broken, and in need of love and repair. *"Not enough"* doesn't encourage us to move toward each other, but rather shoves us further down into our personal pits of darkness.

"I feel like I'm not good (smart, attractive, gifted, etc.) enough," can be true from time to time. *"I'm not enough,"* is a lie.

Again, feelings are real, but they are not necessarily reality.

Instead of telling yourself, *"I'm not enough,"* you must find your own *enough*. More on this later.

On to another lie we often swallow...

CHAPTER SEVEN
I'M ALONE

"*I'M ALONE.*"
This lie has many expressions too.
"*It's all up to me.*"
"*It's me against the world.*"
"*No one understands me.*"

WE FEEL ALONE.

When most of us say, *"I'm alone,"* what we really mean is *"I feel alone."* The distinction between these two statements is huge.

"I'm alone" means there's no one else. You're solo and isolated. It's just you, period.

"I feel alone," means it seems like no one else is in this with you. You might be surrounded by other people, but you feel isolated and on your own. No one else knows what you're thinking or feeling. No one else can completely understand or perfectly relate. You're connected to other people, but you feel lonely.

Again, these are feelings. *Feeling are real, but they are not necessarily reality.*

In whatever you might be going through at any given time, you might feel alone, but someone else is going through it too — or has been through it before. The truth is that we're all walking around experiencing our own individual degrees of loneliness. There's no one in our hearts except, well, us. We don't even know our own minds and hearts well, so how can we expect someone else to?

And in our digital age, we experience all kinds of connection through our screens and devices, but studies indicate we *feel* more alone than ever before. *Alone together* might be a phrase that aptly describes us.

And yet, if we pay attention, there are usually a few people willing to enter our loneliness and share it with us. When this happens, we get to share their loneliness too.

Feeling alone isn't weird. It's human.

You might feel alone, but you never are. We're in this together. Again, we need each other — badly.

On to another lie many believe...

CHAPTER EIGHT
I'M DAMAGED

"*I'M DAMAGED.*"
This lie, like all the others, comes in other forms too.
"I'll never be whole."
"I'll never be a complete person."
"I'll never succeed."
"I'll always be less than everyone else."
"I'm beyond repair — a lost cause."
"I'm hopeless and beyond help."

WE'RE ALL DAMAGED.

Truthfully, we're all damaged. We've all been hurt and wounded, even if we have stellar families and rock-solid childhoods. This world is tough. We all get hit, some of us over and over again. We've all been bruised and dented along the way.

But some of us see ourselves a bit like Humpty-Dumpty. We're cracked, broken, and even smashed. We can't imagine anyone or anything being able to put us back together again.

Perhaps we don't see ourselves as shattered, but rather damaged enough to never be able to do what we want to do or be who we want to be. Many of us feel trapped, tied down, or severely limited.

Again, the truth is we're all damaged. We're all limited. Our tendency is to compare our wounds. Mine are worse than yours. His are worse than mine. Hers are worse than his, etc. We get stuck.

If we buy into this lie deep enough and for long enough, we can feel hopeless and beyond help.

We all need help. We all need repair. If we pay attention and are aware of it, we can help one another heal and succeed.

Again, success is not perfection. That's beyond all of us. We'll talk more about success and what it is and isn't later.

Damaged? Yes.

Beyond help, repair, and hope? No. Far from it.

Here's another lie many of us struggle with...

CHAPTER NINE
I'M INVISIBLE

"*I'M INVISIBLE.*"
 Almost everyone I know feels this way sometimes. It goes something like this...
 "*No one notices me.*"
 "*It's like I'm not even here.*"
 "*People look at me, but no one sees me.*"
 "*I wonder if they even know I exist.*"
 Invisible. Unseen. Unnoticed. Unheard. That's frustrating and painful. And lonely.

FEELING INVISIBLE, BUT HUNGRY TO SEEN.

Some of us, perhaps because of abuse, want to be invisible. To be noticed means to be focused on, and that never turned out well for us.

Others of us are so used to being left out that we make ourselves invisible. We move along the periphery. We literally will people not to see or notice us. We relish anonymity and being able to fly under the radar. Yet something in our hearts warns us that this is not good. Deep down we hunger to seen and noticed.

Still others of us are so used to being in the limelight that we've forgotten who we are. We play the popularity card well. We enjoy the attention, but over time we discover that no one seems interested in the deeper parts of us. Though noticed and fawned over, the *"real us"* gets glossed over. We can lose our sense of who we are. We become invisible underneath the attractive exterior. Vibrant and popular, we can be slowly dying on the inside.

Invisible.

Most of us struggle with this on some level. Imagine this. A group of people walking along, talking, laughing, and seemingly enjoying each other, while deep down each one struggles with his or her own set of insecurities. That's us. That's you. That's the human race.

One of the keys to becoming visible is to allow ourselves to be seen. Do you let yourself — who you really are inside — be seen? By whom?

It's hard to embrace life and love and remain invisible. More on this later.

Now, on to another lie...

CHAPTER TEN
I'M UGLY

"*I'M UGLY.*"
This lie also takes various forms.
"*I have to look like this or that to do this or that.*"
"*I'm too thin, heavy, tall, or short.*"
"*I'm not attractive enough for that, or for him, or for her.*"
"*I don't have the right clothes.*"
"*I can't compete with looks like that.*"

LIVING IN AN APPEARANCE-ORIENTED WORLD.

We live in a media-centered, appearance-oriented world. We seem to care less about the backstory than about how things appear. We look in the mirror and decide whether we like what we see. And what we like is usually based on someone else's idea of what is acceptable, attractive, beautiful, or handsome.

On top of this, appearance-oriented beauty tends to be trendy. This body shape is in, while that one is out. A couple of years down the road, it's reversed. Hairstyles, clothes, cars, possessions, language, and values all tend to be trendy. Wait a while, and something will change. All this appearance mania keeps us chasing our tails and never content with who we are and what is.

Are you what you see in the mirror? Yes, that's your *appearance*. But we both know there's much more to you than that. Sadly, appearance often counts for more than it's worth in our world.

Most of us try hard not to be ugly. Sometimes that's hard to do when definitions of attractiveness seem to change overnight and are different from person to person and place to place.

True attractiveness must be more than this.

Yes, it is. More on this later.

And now on to the final lie we'll talk about.

CHAPTER ELEVEN
"IT'S ALL SOMEONE ELSE'S FAULT"

"*It's all someone else's fault.*"
Here are some common variations of this lie:
"*It's their fault I'm like this.*"
"*I'm not responsible for being this way.*"
"*It's not my fault (it's never my fault).*"
"*Someone's to blame for this, somehow, somewhere.*"
"*I can't help it. These are the cards I was dealt.*"

THE BLAME GAME

Ah, the blame game. We're good at this. We point the finger at others quickly and readily. We've developed blame-shifting into an art form.

Some of us pass off responsibility because we don't want to get in trouble. Others of us have been hurt so badly that we just can't afford any more pain, even if it's our own doing. Still others of us frantically try to keep up the appearance of perfection by deflecting unwanted attention to others.

Many of us are ready to see blame placed elsewhere if it gives us a pass on discipline, judgment, or anything uncomfortable. This is what is modeled for us so often by those we follow, watch, or idolize. Not many own up to their own words or actions if honesty might shake their popularity or damage their image.

Owning up to what we've done and said takes guts. Serious courage.

And so, the blame continues. We're all guilty of this. I know I am. Everything is not your fault. Not by a long shot. But you are responsible for your own thoughts, words, and actions.

More on this later.

WHERE WE'VE BEEN AND WHERE WE'RE GOING

In this section, we've focused on the lies we tend to believe. A lot of the pain in our lives comes from these untruths. Here are some big ones we've talked about so far:

"I'm unlovable."
"I'm worthless."
"I'm not enough."
"I'm alone."
"I'm damaged."
"I'm invisible."
"I'm ugly."
"It's all someone else's fault."

Look inside. Back up and observe your life. Which of these lies have influenced you? Circle them or write them down here. Feel free to put them in your own words.

_____
_____
_____

We all live out what we truly believe (as opposed to what we say we believe). Look at your life. What does how you live say about what you believe about you?

_____
_____
_____

What you believe about you may be the most important thing about you. It will influence everything — and determine a lot.

Run your eyes over those lies again. Let them sink in.

> Say it with me:
> *"These are lies."*

These are the enemies of your heart. They hold you back. They keep you stuck. Unearth them. Be aware of them. Stare them down.

It's time to think differently. It's time to fight. Fight for yourself and those you love by fighting for your own heart.

It's not enough to be aware of these lies and their power in your life. You must unplug them. You do that by replacing them with the truth.

But first, you have to discover what the truth is and embrace it.

Your heart is about to shift. Can you feel it?

Read on.

Many of our struggles come from lies we've been fed and believed over the years. These debilitating lies are no longer welcome. To these foes of our hearts, we say, "Look out, lies. We're coming for you." We are Difference Makers.

PART THREE:
EMBRACING THE GOOD STUFF
(Believing Truths that Propel You Forward)

IN THE LAST SECTION, WE exposed some lies many of us believe. I believed many of them and still struggle with some. These lies mess with our minds, hearts, and relationships. We can't afford to let them live comfortably in our hearts.

How do you battle lies, or even get rid of them?

You replace them with the truth.

Let's talk about the truth.

CHAPTER 12
I'M VALUABLE

WE TALK ABOUT HUMAN RIGHTS. We get passionate about equality and justice. What's the underlying principle for these things?

Every person has intrinsic value.

By intrinsic value, I mean that a person does not have to say anything, do anything, or accomplish anything to be of value. A human being's value is automatic, regardless of race, education, appearance, income, age, health, or any other condition or situation.

Humans are of great value, period.

You are of great value, far more than you know. And this is apart from anything you've ever thought, done, said, or accomplished.

HOW VALUABLE ARE YOU?

Personally, I believe you are of priceless worth that never diminishes, no matter what happens to you or around you. Your value isn't based on what anyone else does, thinks, or says. Your worth is intrinsic and measureless.

Consider this: There has never been another person exactly like you in the entire history of the human race — even if you're a twin. There will never be another person exactly like you in the future. You are absolutely unique. One-of-a-kind.

And out of all the times and places where you could have been born and lived, you are here, now. You occupy a completely unique space and time in human history.

That's stunning. Amazing. Special.

You are valuable beyond description. The sooner you embrace this truth, the more peace and joy you will find down the road.

Of course, what I've just said is true not only for you, but for all those around you and everyone you meet.

Do you want to begin to experience how valuable you are? Treat others as valuable.

When you're with family, friends, or even strangers, look into their eyes for a moment and let it sink in. Let your mind dwell on the truth. *"Unique in all of human history. One-of-a-kind. Special. And out of all the times and places they could have been born and lived, they are here with me, now."*

> *Every person — special and unique.*
> *Every relationship — one-of-a-kind.*
> *Every conversation — a once-in-a-lifetime opportunity.*

MIRROR TIME

You are valuable.

Go and stand in front of a mirror. Say it.

"I'm valuable."

Say it again.

Look into your own eyes. Do you believe it?

When the *"I'm worthless"* thoughts come, don't let them sneak in unnoticed. Call them out.

"Lie!"

Then, speak the truth.

"I'm valuable. I'm one-of-a-kind. I'm unique."

Now, pay attention to those around you. Look at them and say to yourself, *"Valuable. One-of-a-kind. Unique."*

Practice this. Make it a habit. Tell yourself the truth about yourself and others.

The battle begins in your mind. Thoughts lead to actions.

Whatever you think about repeatedly begins to work its way into your life.

CONSIDER:

Think about yourself and your life. In what ways do you see yourself as valuable?

_____
_____
_____

Do you question your value? In what ways?

_____
_____
_____

How might accepting and believing that you are inherently valuable (apart from anything you think, say, or do) change the way you look at life and the way you live? Try to think of some specific examples.

_____
_____
_____

Difference Makers are of inherent, priceless value. You are a Difference Maker.

Whatever you think about yourself leaks out into your life. Embrace your value. You and everyone else will benefit.

CHAPTER 13
I'M NOT PERFECT

YOU HAVE EXPECTATIONS OF YOURSELF. Lots of them. You expect certain things of yourself at home, at work, with friends, and in your family.

You have expectations of others too. You expect to be talked to and treated in a certain way by certain people.

Those around you also have expectations, and some of them are about you. They expect you to think, talk, and behave a certain way in certain situations.

Expectations are sneaky. Like a virus, they come in undetected and begin to mess with our lives.

THE EXPECTATION OF PERFECTION

Most of us expect some form of perfection — from ourselves and from others. We expect things to be a certain way or work out like this or that. The trouble is that situations, conversations, relationships, and life don't pan out the way we anticipate. We get surprised. Disappointment strikes. And sometimes the disappointment is painful.

Who wants to be disappointed?

Who wants to be disappointing?

It would be nice if we could identify just what our expectations are of ourselves and other people. If we did that, then we could see better how realistic our expectations are and how likely they are to be fulfilled.

Author Donald Miller said, "When you stop expecting people to be perfect, you can like them for who they are."

I've certainly found that to be true. Conversely, when you stop expecting yourself to be perfect, you can like yourself for who you are.

Imagine the freedom you could give yourself — and others — if you hugged this truth tightly. No one is perfect. We're all flawed. Life isn't about becoming perfect. Life is about embracing our imperfections and using them for good.

You're not perfect. That's okay.
You'll never be perfect. That's okay too.

Growth and healing begin when you accept yourself for who you are, where you are.

MIRROR TIME

Go to that mirror again. Look yourself in the eye. Say it.

"I'm not perfect, and that's okay."

How did that feel?

Say it again.

Now, say this.

"I'll never be perfect, and that's okay too."

Pause. Let that sink in.

Say it again.

And now, say, *"I release myself from having to be perfect."*

How did that feel?

Say it again.

"I release myself from having to be perfect."

Now, one more time, adding one more sentence.

"I release myself from having to be perfect. I'll be myself instead."

Think about that. Say it one more time.

Practice this. Practice doesn't make perfect, but practice does tend to make things permanent.

Now, take a moment and think about someone you know. Your spouse, girlfriend, boyfriend, or mate. One of your children. A parent. A friend or co-worker. Maybe even someone you don't like.

See them in your mind, and say this, *"You're not perfect either."*

Now add, *"You'll never be perfect."*

And then say the real clincher, *"So I will stop expecting you to be different than you are."*

Pause a moment, and then try that again.

"You're not perfect either. You'll never be perfect. So, I will stop expecting you to be different than you are."

You might feel a little dumb, but the more you look at yourself and say these things, the better it will feel. Our hearts tend to believe what we feed them.

Feed your heart the truth.

You're not perfect. That's reality, and that's okay.

You can quit trying to be perfect and just be yourself instead. After all, that's all you can do. As Irish poet and playwright Oscar Wilde said, *"Be yourself; everyone else is already taken."*

As you let yourself off the perfection hook, be sure to extend that kindness to others too. Let the perfection expectation go. Throw it far from you.

The goal is not perfection. Your target is to be the best version of yourself possible.

What does that mean? More on that later.

CONSIDER:

Do you feel like you have to get things *right* or *perfect*? Give some examples.

_____

_____

_____

What message in your past seems to be the driving force behind your perfectionism? Don't overthink this. Write down what comes to mind.

_____
_____
_____

Do you expect perfection from others? If so, in what areas? What do others do that irritates you? What do you tend to be most critical about in others' lives?

_____
_____
_____

Can you see how granting yourself and others the freedom to be imperfect is a healthy and empowering gift? How can you see your life changing if you were free from all burdens of perfectionism?

_____
_____
_____

> ***Your target is not perfection. Instead, be the best version of yourself possible.***

CHAPTER 14
IT'S NOT ABOUT MY APPEARANCE

As we said before, we live in an appearance-oriented world — a digital world of perpetual selfies, filters, and effects.

We tend to judge and be judged based on our outside at the moment. Sadly, those who are deemed attractive often get treated better. On the other hand, attractiveness can also bring unwelcome attention from unwanted sources. Looking good can be a double-edged sword.

Of course, we know that we are more than our appearance. All it takes is one accident, and faces or bodies can be permanently marred. We should care how we look, but if we're wise, we'll invest in our hearts.

IT'S ABOUT YOUR HEART.

Over 3000 years ago, a wise king named Solomon said, *"Guard you heart. It is the spring from which all your life flows."*

Your heart is your most prized possession. It houses your secret thoughts, desires, and hopes. It longs to love and be loved. It looks for connection, meaning, and purpose. It prizes things like kindness, humility, and true strength.

Your heart is who you are.

Guard your heart. That phrase implies that the inner core of your being is under assault. There are things out there that would rob you of love, joy, peace, and hope. You can't afford to let that happen.

Your heart is meant to be exercised. It is most healthy when it expresses love and care. It thrives on service to others. Ironically, service to others is excellent medicine for your own wounds.

The inside matters. Your heart is all-important. You must nurture it, take care of it, and give it the exercise it needs. Reach out. Care. Love. Serve.

As stunning as external beauty can be, it is nothing compared to the ravishing power of a humble, service-seeking heart.

Do you put as much effort into your heart as you do into your body, face, or outward appearance?

People who leverage the power of their hearts are some of the most powerful influencers around.

Do you consider yourself less than attractive? By what standards? In whose eyes? What ruler are you measuring with?

Attractiveness, when we're talking about physical appearance, is based on current popular opinion. The key word is *opinion*. That makes it subjective. The old adage, *"Beauty is in the eye of the beholder,"* is true indeed.

Ugly is a comparison-based word. Ugly compared to what? Compared to whom? When?

You're not perfect, but you're valuable. You're unique and more important than you know. No one can fill your place in life. It's reserved for you. Only you can fill that seat.

The key to filling your place well is your heart. It is the essence of who you are. Take care of it. Feed it carefully. Exercise it well.

MIRROR TIME

Now, it's mirror time.

Look yourself in the eye and say, *"I am not my appearance."*

Think about that. Now, say it again.

"I am not my appearance."

What are you thinking right now? How does that statement strike you?

Now say this: *"My heart is who I am."*

Pause. Now, say it again.

"My heart is who I am."
Do you believe it?
Say it again.
"My heart is who I am."
Now say, *"I will protect and care for my heart."*

What's true about you is also true about those around you. Think for a moment about someone you know well. Close your eyes. See them in your mind.

Say to yourself, *"They are not their appearance. Their heart is who they are."*

Try this when you're in public. Look at those around you. Remind yourself that their heart is the most important thing about them. Their heart is who they are.

It's time to stop judging yourself based on your appearance. It's time to quit evaluating others this way too. Learn to look past the outside to the heart within.

Things are often not what they appear. People are often different than what they seem. Dig deeper. *Start living from your heart.*

CONSIDER:

Do you feel others judge you based on your appearance? How so?
_____
_____
_____

Take a moment and look inside. What's important to you in life? Make a short list.
_____
_____
_____

How would you describe your heart — who you really are?

_____
_____
_____

> ***Live from your heart, and it will show up everywhere. Your heart is who you are.***

CHAPTER 15
I CAN HEAL

Earlier in this book, we talked about how we all feel damaged in some way. We've all been wounded. We've all been disappointed. Our hearts have been hit, perhaps even broken.

Some of us have experienced sexual or physical abuse. Others have been victims of violent crime. Still others have been rejected, neglected, or even abandoned. Some of us have harmed ourselves. Some have considered suicide.

Our wounds go deep. You feel yours. I feel mine. Sometimes, the wounds can take over. Life can become dark. All we can see is pain. We assume that it will always be this way.

That's the key. When in pain, we assume that the pain will continue. We think that the way things are now is the way they will be forever.

Thankfully, this is not true. Now is not forever. Things can change. We can change. We can heal.

YOU CAN HEAL.

Your wounds do not define you. You are not your wounds. You are not what has happened to you. You are not what others have done and said. You are not your failures and mistakes.

You can heal.

Healing doesn't just happen. Most of the time, it takes a decision on your part. You must decide you want to heal. You must take the steps toward healing. Your heart is powerful. Your decisions are huge.

When I was in high school, my swim coach had a favorite motivational phrase. Turned out, it was more of a life wisdom phrase. He said it a lot. He posted it everywhere. I even carried a card in my wallet with this phrase on it:

"*Garbage in, garbage out.*"

What I choose to put in greatly influences — and can even determine — what comes out.

If I put garbage in, I can expect garbage out.

If I receive lies and let them take root, I end up living them out. They will shape and perhaps even destroy my heart.

If I take in truth and embrace it, truth will flow out of my heart and into my thoughts, words, and actions.

If I put health and healing in, I can expect health and healing out.

Garbage in, garbage out.
Good in, good out.

It's my choice. It's your choice. Our daily decisions matter.

No one else can fill your space. The world needs you. Make the choice to heal. Make that choice now, and tomorrow, and the day after that.

This isn't easy. It's a battle. Healing doesn't happen overnight. Change like this takes time.

Time.

In our digital age, we don't wait well. We're impatient. Time is often the enemy. The faster, the better. If things aren't immediate or instantaneous, we're off and on to something else.

Healing takes time. There are no shortcuts. There is no magic button. Your heart is worth fighting for. Fight for those you care about and love by fighting for yourself.

We're talking about your life here. You are your heart. *Make the decision to heal.*

MIRROR TIME

Get in front of a mirror. Look yourself in the eye.

Think about your wounds. Think about how you have been hurt. Think for a moment about the frustrations, rejections, losses, and disappointments you've endured.

Now, say, *"I can heal."*

Pause, and then say it again.

"I can heal."

You may not believe this yet, and that's okay. Your mind might need to get used to the idea.

Say it again.

"I can heal."

Okay. Take a deep breath. Look again into your own eyes, and say, *"I choose to heal."*

Let that settle in, and then say it again.

"I choose to heal."

Tell yourself the truth as often as you can. You can heal. And then make the choice to heal, again and again.

"I can heal. I choose to heal."

Of course, healing doesn't occur in a vacuum. Because you're designed for relationship and wired for connection, you won't be able to heal alone. People will make all the difference in your life. They will be key in your healing and growth.

Your healing — and the quality of your life — will be greatly influenced by the people you choose to be around and surround yourself with. This is huge. Massive.

More on that later.

CONSIDER:

Think about the wounds you've had in life: losses, deaths, rejections, disappointments, failures, abuse, etc. List some of them here.

_____

_____

_____

Do you believe you can heal from these things?

___

Does the *garbage-in-garbage-out* idea make sense to you? Can you see this principle (what you put in determines what comes out) at work in your life?

___

What kind of person do you want to be? Write a brief description.

___

What kinds of things do you need to be putting into your life and heart to make this possible?

___

No one is beyond repair. No one. You can heal. Choose healing.

CHAPTER 16
I'M SIGNIFICANT

ONE-OF-A-KIND. UNIQUE IN ALL OF human history. Special beyond calculation.

That's you.

You matter.

Your thoughts count.

Your words are powerful.

Your actions send ripple effects into the lives of all those around you.

What goes on inside you is massively important. Your heart is a priceless treasure.

NO ONE CAN FILL YOUR SPACE BUT YOU.

You matter. You have far more influence than you know.

This is the opposite of being worthless. It is also the opposite of being invisible. You occupy a crucial place in time, space, and history. No one can fill this space but you.

Of course, there are many times when you probably feel you don't matter. Join the club. I still feel this way from time to time. Remember that feelings are real, but they are not necessarily reality. If even those around you seem to be treating you like you don't matter, the message itself is a lie.

No matter what happens or what anyone else says or does, you matter — period.

Your worth and importance aren't dependent on what happens to you or around you. Your value isn't dependent on what others say or do. Don't entrust your heart to the lies swirling around you. Focus your attention squarely on the truth.

The truth is you matter. You are crucially important and massively significant. You are here for a reason, and no one else can play your particular role.

Here is another bit of truth. You will never become who you could be unless you accept, believe, and begin to live out the truth that you're significant.

Again, it doesn't matter what anyone else says or does. Your heart must conquer this. Do these things hurt sometimes? Yes. Do you feel alone and isolated at times? Yes. Are there times when you feel like no one understands you? You bet. Is life tough, confusing, and full of seemingly impossible challenges? Absolutely.

Life isn't about being comfortable. Life is about overcoming.

Success isn't measured by the size of bank accounts, houses, cars, or an attractive partner. In the end, success isn't defined by grades, social circles, talent, or getting what you think you want.

In the long run, success is measured by how much you live from your heart. This means living out the truth that you matter. Living from your heart also means living out the truth that all those around you matter too.

This is the math of life. If you start treating others like they matter, you begin to believe that you matter too. If you treat yourself like you matter, you will naturally begin to extend the same gift to others too. As you begin to see those around you, you'll discover that others are seeing you as well.

Live from your heart, and the hearts around you will begin to respond.

But even if those around you don't respond well, you still matter. The truth does not change.

Once you start to live the truth, it begins to permeate your heart and powerfully influence how you think, speak, and act. Over time, as living like you matter becomes a habit, you'll begin to feel it and experience this truth more and more.

Again, we're talking about accepting, believing, and living the truth. You're significant. All those around you are significant. Period.

MIRROR TIME

Let's head to the mirror.

Take a moment and gaze into your own eyes. Take your time.
When you feel ready, say, *"I matter."*
Let that sink in.
Say it again.
"I matter."
Now, add, *"I'm significant."*
"I matter. I'm significant."
Now, say it again, adding one more phrase.
"I matter. I'm significant. And I will live like it."
One more time.
"I matter. I'm significant. And I will live like it."
Take a deep breath. Close your eyes. Think of someone you really care about. See them in your mind's eye.
Say, *"They matter."*
Say it again.
"They matter."
Add one more phrase.
"They matter. They're significant."
Take another deep breath, and then think of someone you don't particularly like. See them in your mind.
Now say, *"They matter too."*
Say it again.
"They matter too."
Add one more phrase.
"They matter too. They're significant."
For a moment, imagine treating everyone you meet like they matter. Real success flows from becoming the Difference Maker you were destined to be. And becoming that Difference Maker is a result of you accepting, believing, and living the truth, over time.

Imagine being able to treat each person you meet like they're significant. For many of them, you just made their day. Truth is powerful. They have felt it from you, and the ripple effects have now begun in their life.

Every contact matters. Every interaction matters. Our hearts are always there, influencing and being influenced by what is said and done. Every pebble and rock thrown into the pond of life matters.

If you treat those you meet like they're significant, that kindness tends to boomerang back to you. Most people respond well to being treated as human beings who are one-of-a-kind special. Every heart needs to be seen. Most hearts respond back in some way that says, *"Thank you. You matter too."*

But even if some people don't respond the way you might hope, your heart will still benefit from living the truth that we all matter.

You're significant.
All those around you are significant.
Everyone you will ever meet is significant.
Accept it. Believe it. Live it. Practice it today,
tomorrow, and the day after that.

As you make living like we all matter a habit, your heart will begin to feel this truth on a deeper level.

So often we go at things backwards. We feel a certain way, which causes us to think a certain way, which then produces certain words and actions. If we think about this as if it were a train, the order would be:

Feelings — Thoughts — Words — Actions

Feelings are the engine driving this train.

Truth rarely gets lived out when we allow feelings to drive our decisions. If you want to live well and be the Difference Maker you can be, your train needs to shift some cars around.

A truth-living Difference Maker's train looks like this:

Truth — Thoughts — Words — Actions — Feelings

Let's think about this using the truth that you — and all those around you — are significant.

First, the truth that you and everyone else matters influences your thoughts. Your thoughts lead to words and actions. The more you live out the truth that everyone matters, the more you begin to feel like you do indeed matter.

Make sense?

I know, I know. Easy to say. Hard to do.

Yes, you're right.

Life is not about being comfortable.
Life is not about getting what we think we want.
Life is about discovering, embracing, and living the truth.
Life is about overcoming the negative junk
that happens to and around us.
Life is about learning to tackle obstacles by
guarding and living from your heart.
Life is about giving your heart what it needs in order
to impact this broken and needy world for good.

You matter — far more than you know.

You're a Difference Maker.

CONSIDER:

What are some of the things that cause you to question your significance? How others treat you? What they say? What you say to yourself about you?

_____

_____

_____

Are there ways you can treat others as the significant, one-of-a-kind individuals they are? What will you do and how?

Family:_____

Friends:_____

Co-workers:_____

Previously invisible people:_____

You're significant. So are they. Live the truth. Be the Difference Maker you are.

You're more significant than you realize. So is everyone else.

CHAPTER 17
I'M LOVABLE

Yes, you are lovable.
Let's think about the truth we've covered.

You are valuable.
You're not perfect and that's okay.
You can heal.
It's not about your appearance. It's about your heart.
You matter. You're significant.

Let those things sink in again.
How could you not be lovable?

YOU ARE LOVED.

Here's another bit of truth: you are loved. Yes, you are. By someone. Most likely by a lot of people.

Do you always feel loved? Probably not. But that's a feeling and not necessarily reality.

Are there times when you feel like no one really loves you? Perhaps. Again, that's a feeling and not actually the truth.

Does anyone love you perfectly?

No. That's impossible. None of us are perfect. Imperfect people can't love perfectly.

But we can love. And we can get really good at it, too.

It's natural to want someone to love you perfectly, but that's not going to happen – at least not by another mere human being. Let go of that expectation. Accept the reality that we live in a broken world where all of us are stumbling along, trying to make sense of things and get what we think our needs are met somehow.

We love imperfectly.

Do yourself a favor and release other people from having to love you perfectly. Don't expect them to know your heart and read your mind. They can't. If you expect perfection from others, you're setting yourself up for disappointment, anger, and misery.

And while you're at it, release yourself from having to get things perfect in your relationships. It's not going to happen. Set your sights on loving others as best you know how.

LET'S THINK ABOUT LOVE FOR A MOMENT.

What is love anyway?

As we said before, it's far more than an emotion. Love affects us emotionally, but it's way beyond a mere mood or feeling.

More than a noun, love might be best described as a verb. It's action-oriented.

Love is the action resulting from thinking about someone and then speaking and acting for their benefit. Love is not a feeling, but a way of thinking, speaking and acting that results in various emotions.

You might not feel loved, but I guarantee you there are people around you who are thinking about you and speaking and acting for your benefit and in your best interests.

Accept it. You are loved. Believe it. It's true.

Think for a moment. Who is most likely thinking about you on a regular basis and speaking and acting to make your life better and help you grow?

Keep thinking. Make a list. Don't be skimpy, either.

PEOPLE MOST LIKELY THINKING ABOUT ME AND WORKING FOR MY GOOD:

1. _____
2. _____
3. _____
4. _____
5. _____

LOVE IS A VERB.

We tend to equate love with emotional chemistry and romance. Attraction is important, but it's also just one aspect of love.

Let me come back to something we've said. Love is best understood as a verb, rather than a noun.

Let's think about that for a moment. *Love is a verb.*

Perhaps, then, we should think about *what it means to be loving rather than what love is.*

Life is full of tough decisions. Over the years, I've heard, *"I just want to do the right thing,"* thousands of times. I don't know about you, but sometimes the *right thing* is hard for me to decipher.

What if life is not about being *right* or doing the *right* thing? *What if life is about being loving?*

What if, when faced with a tough decision (or any decision for that matter), we asked, *"What would be loving in this case?"* or *"How can I express love to this person in this situation?"*

I think that would change some things. I know it's changed things for me. For one thing, decision-making is much easier. For imperfect people — as we all are — figuring out the *right* thing can be confusing sometimes. But everyone can easily come up with something that would be loving.

Again, we don't love perfectly, but we can still love well.

You are lovable. This is the truth.
But it gets even better. You are loved.

Yes, you are. By more people than you realize. People all around you are thinking about you. They are speaking and acting for your benefit and in your interests. Love is not about giving you what you think you want, but about making sure you have what you need.

You are loved. More than you realize.

MIRROR TIME

It's mirror time. Find one. Look into your own eyes.

Say it.

"I am lovable."

Now say, *"I am loved."*

Pause. Breathe. Say it again.

"I am lovable. I am loved."

Say it again — as many times as you want to.

Again, you may not feel it, but that doesn't change the truth. *You are lovable. You are loved.*

Now, think about someone you know. You choose. Anyone. See them in your mind.

Now say, *"You are lovable. You are loved."*

Say it again.

What you tell yourself matters. Garbage in, garbage out. Truth in, truth out.

Keep putting the truth into your heart and watch what happens over time.

You will know better how much you are loved. You will be more loving to others. And, you will feel more and more loved in return.

Remember the truth train. Truth is the engine, followed by thoughts, words, actions, and feelings.

Truth – Thoughts – Words – Actions — Feelings

Let truth drive your life. You'll be glad you did.

What's the truth? *You are lovable. You are loved.*

CONSIDER:

Can you think of examples in your life where you are loved, but don't always feel like you are?

_____

_____

_____

What are you going to tell yourself about this?

_____

_____

_____

Think of three people in your life — one person you feel very close to, one you're struggling with right now, and one acquaintance.

1. Person I'm close to:

2. Someone I'm struggling with:

3. An acquaintance:

Think of each of the above individually and ask yourself, *"How can I be loving to them the next time I see them?"*

Don't shoot for the moon. Keep it simple. Simple words and actions that express concern and kindness can go a long, long way.

Difference Makers know they are loved. They learn to think, speak, and act for the good of others. They know they're imperfect, but they don't let that stop them from loving others well.

Love is a verb. Difference Makers know this. They're focused on loving well and getting better at it all the time.

> *Garbage in, garbage out. Truth in, truth out. You are lovable. You are loved.*

CHAPTER 18
I'M FAR FROM ALONE

You're far from alone.
    Yes, you'll feel alone. Maybe a lot. But that's a feeling. The truth is something different.

Yes, there are times when you're physically alone and there's no one else immediately around you, but you're never alone when it comes to your heart. No matter what you're going through, someone else has been through or is going through something similar.

We're all individuals, but none of us travel the road of life alone. We never have. Other people have been with us since we took our first breath. We grew up interacting with others, and at first, we were dependent on those around us for everything. We received, and received, and received. Along the way, we learned to give. Whether we could express it or not, we began naturally living the truth that life is a dynamic combo of giving and receiving.

We discovered that we needed time alone. We also knew we needed other people. Even those of us who describe ourselves as loners are connected to others. We're all far more attached than we know. We're part of a massive network of people and relationships.

WHAT DO WE DO WITH LONELINESS?

Yes, we feel alone at times. As we said before, no other human being knows the depths of our hearts or the exact thoughts of our mind. These are ours, and ours alone. That's special, but it can also be lonely.

So, what do we do?

We share.

We let people in on what we're thinking and feeling. We give others access to our hearts.

Of course, not everyone should have access to our innermost being. There are people out there who are toxic. They're negative and critical. They spew their angst and discontent on those around them. They slice you, dice you, and then throw you away. They gossip, belittle, and demean. They are masters at rumor-creation.

Guard your heart. Don't trust untrustworthy people. Don't give toxic people access to your heart. As much as possible, limit your exposure to them and their influences.

Thankfully, there are plenty of non-toxic people out there. We're all imperfect and we all mess up in relationships. We say things we shouldn't and do things that we later regret. Again, don't expect perfection, because you won't find it — either in yourself or in others.

Amid all our imperfection, there are some safe people out there. These people are gems — diamonds in the rough.

WHAT'S A SAFE PERSON LIKE?

Though they are imperfect and mess up from time to time, on the whole, safe people do the following:

- Accept you as you are.
- Show genuine interest in you — your life and your heart.
- Respect your boundaries.
- Listen well.
- Say helpful, loving things.
- Put your heart at ease.

You feel safe in their presence. That's huge. There is no healing or growth for any of us without a sense of safety.

Who are the safe people in your life?

Think. They're out there. Who are they?

You might know some of them well. Others might be on the periphery of your daily life. There might be others that you don't really know, but from watching them you get the sense that they can be trusted.

Make a quick list. Of the people you know, whom do you sense might be safe?

_____

_____

_____

These people will make all the difference in your life. Get around them as much as you can. Let them love you by being safe harbors amid your storms. These people will be *for* you, no matter what.

Follow this logic with me.

You're wired for connection and designed for relationships.

You're made to love and be loved.

You're important and significant, one-of-a-kind in all of human history.

You have a unique space to occupy and a crucial role to play.

Therefore, people will make all the difference in your life, one way or another.

It's paramount — crucial — critical - that you get around people who take your heart seriously and help propel you forward.

It's been said that we become a composite of the five people we're around the most. Whom we offer our hearts to is massively important.

Your heart is who you are. Choose your companions wisely.

Toxic people are your role models for how NOT to be.

People who are not helpful, who drag you down, are not wise choices for close friends.

People who hold you back rather than propelling you forward aren't worth investing your heart with.

Safe people — no matter how old they are or what their role in your life is — are your companions, mentors, and guides. They are the shoulders that you stand on as you become the Difference Maker you were meant to be.

Identify your safe people. Find some more. They are the people who will affirm the truths we've talked about. Safe people will tell you with their attitudes, words, and actions that…

- You are valuable.
- You are imperfect but can grow.
- You are wounded but can heal.
- You are more than your appearance.
- Your heart is your most prized possession.
- You are loved and lovable.
- You are never, ever alone.

WHAT? NO SAFE PEOPLE IN SIGHT?

Some of you are reading this and thinking, *"I don't know many safe people. What do I do?"*

The best way to find safe people is to become one.

Yes, you read that right.

The best way to find someone safe is to be safe yourself.

Safe people attract each other like magnets. They recognize each other almost instantly and intuitively.

If you want to find good, safe people to help launch you to being an amazing Difference Maker, set your sights on being a safe person yourself.

Here's some great news. As you accept the truths we've talked about, believe them, and begin to live them out, you will naturally become a safe person.

Here's how it works.

As you accept and live out the truth that you are valuable, one-of-a-kind, and unique, you begin to see others as such too. This leads to greater respect, less angst, and healthier relationships.

As you believe and live the truth that you're not perfect but you can heal, you begin to extend that same kindness to others. People relax in your presence because you don't expect them to be perfect.

As you embrace the truth that you are more than your appearance and that your heart is what matters, you begin to view those around you this way. They begin to see that you are non-judgmental and accepting. They naturally draw closer to you.

As you accept and live the truth that you matter and are worth seeing, you will find yourself seeing others this way too. People are drawn to those who see past their appearance to their hearts.

As you believe and live the truth that you are lovable and loved, it changes the way you see others — especially those who are hurting. Other wounded hearts will come knocking. They see something they like in you. They sense safety.

As you embrace and live the truth that you are far from alone, others will sense the security in you. They long for that security themselves, and they'll naturally be drawn to you.

And, viola! You suddenly realize you have become a Difference Maker.

Amazing. Stunning. Downright miraculous.

Then it dawns on you.

"Oh my. The sky's the limit. The more I accept, believe, and live the truth, the more I become who I really am. The more impact I have. The more of a Difference Maker I become."

Yes.

Now, let me give a disclaimer.

Everyone is a Difference Maker.

Yes, everyone.

We all have influence. We exercise that influence, every day.

The question is, *"What kind of influence are we having?"*

> *"You are a Difference Maker. What kind of*
> *Difference Maker do you want to be?"*

Accept the truth. Believe it. Embrace it. Live it. You are far from alone.

You're connected. Your life is a web of people and relationships. You end up becoming a composite of the people you're around the most. Get around people who are living in truth:

- I'm valuable, and so are you.
- I'm imperfect. We all are.
- I can heal. We all can.
- I'm not my appearance, and neither are you.
- My heart matters. So does yours.
- I am lovable and loved. So are you.
- I'm far from alone. We're in this together.

Do this, and you're on your way to some incredible difference-making.

MIRROR TIME

It's mirror time again.

Gaze into your own eyes. See yourself. Know that you are more than your appearance. Your heart is all-important.

Now say, *"I'm far from alone."*

Pause. Let that sink in.

Say it again.

"I'm far from alone."

Now, say, *"I'm far from alone. We're all in this together."*

Say it again.

"I'm far from alone. We're all in this together."

You're connected. Your life is a web.

People will make all the difference.

Invest your heart with those who will propel you forward.

I sense some world-changing difference-making in your future.

CONSIDER:

Make another quick list of the safe people in your life. Don't forget those you don't know well, but sense they are safe and trustworthy.

_____
_____
_____

Are there ways you can reach out and rub shoulders with these people more? How?

_____
_____
_____

Are there less-than-savory or toxic people in your life you need to limit your exposure to? How will you do that? If you can't limit your time with them, how can you better guard your heart?

_____
_____
_____

Let's say it's true that you become a composite of the five people you're around the most. What five people do you want to be influenced by?

_____
_____
_____

Difference Makers find each other. They encourage each other, cheer one another on, and make each other better.

Fill your life with other Difference Makers. You'll be glad you did.

> *You might feel alone, but you never are. Find other Difference Makers and connect with them.*

WHERE WE'VE BEEN AND WHERE WE'RE GOING

In this section, we talked about the importance of you telling yourself the truth.

If you want to be a Difference Maker for good, you'll have to be aware of the lies you've bought into over years. These lies won't go away. Your mind and heart are used to them, and if you're not careful, those lies can slink in and exercise their influence unnoticed.

Expose the lies. Stay on your guard against them. Replace them with the truth.

We've talked about a number of truths in this section.

You are valuable. One-of-a-kind. Unique. There has never been anyone exactly like you, and there never will be again. You are special. Priceless.

You're not perfect, and that's okay. Perfection is beyond us all. Set yourself (and others) free from the expectation that you must always get it right.

You've been wounded, but you can heal. You can heal more than you realize.

You are not your appearance. Your heart is your most prized possession. Focus on your heart.

You matter. You're more significant than you realize. You occupy a unique time and space and have crucial role in the big picture that only you can fill.

You are lovable, and you are loved. Even if your feelings are different, there are always people around you who care and are looking out for your best interests.

You're far from alone. Your life is a web of relationships. People will make all the difference in your life, one way or the other. Find and get around people who will propel you forward toward being the Difference Maker you want to be.

Through all of these truths, there is a general principle of life that needs to noticed. *We tend to receive what we give away.* In other words, what we offer to others tends to boomerang back around to us.

As you live out these truths, you'll find yourself growing and healing. As you live out the truth that those around you are also valuable, imperfect (but essential), wounded (but can heal), and worthy of love, people will notice and be drawn to you. As you share your heart with trustworthy people, and others share their hearts with you, you'll find yourself longing to make more of a positive difference than ever.

Positive impact is contagious. You were made for this.

Accept it. Believe it. Live it.

Difference Maker. That's you.

Difference Makers are aware of lies and expose them.
They seek truth and embrace it.
Difference Makers treat others the way they
themselves want to be treated.
The world will never be the same.
We are Difference Makers.

PART FOUR
HURDLING THE OBSTACLES
(Conquering Things That Can Trip You Up)

Difference-making isn't easy. The best things in life never are.

Difference-making takes courage. You have more than you know. It's time to dig deep.

Difference-making requires patience. There's no key on the keyboard for this. Influence takes place over time.

Difference-making is a battle, and it begins in your mind.

Lies hold you back. Truth propels you forward.

Expose the lies you've believed. Be aware of them. Replace them with the truth. Do this, and you will be on your way to living with more purpose, mission, and impact that you ever thought possible.

You will face other potential enemies in this fight. Here are some of the big ones.

Losses. Big deaths and little deaths.
Anger. Rage.
Fear and anxiety.
Sadness, depression, and suicidal thoughts.

These can be significant challenges indeed. Notice I used the word challenges, not impossibilities.

You will encounter these things. You have already met many of these potential enemies and some of them may have even taken up residence in your mind and heart.

As a Difference Maker, you will learn to not only battle these enemies, but overcome them and use them for good.

Life is about overcoming. Difference Makers embrace this.

CHAPTER 19
Big Deaths, Little Deaths, and Other Bad Stuff

Loss comes in many forms. Rejections. Break-ups. Failures. Divorce. Abuse. Moves. Deaths.

How you think about and respond to these things will make a huge impact on your life and your future. Difference Makers take what happens to and around them and find ways to use it for good.

Sad to say, but studies show that negative experiences tend to carry a lot more weight than positive ones. We all experience loss. Our losses shape us. Some of them can be defining moments in our lives. Traumatic events can skew how we think about life, ourselves, others, and relationships.

What you've been through has impacted you greatly, but it doesn't have to define you.

Did you catch that?

What's happened to you doesn't have to define you.

Unfortunately, many people allow their losses to tell them who they are, how much they're worth, and what they can accomplish. Some losses are so powerful that they become the unseen shadows that hem us in, confining us to small, mediocre lives.

We can't afford to let this happen. We must find ways to use our losses to propel us forward, rather than knuckling under to pain that can deaden our hearts.

So, what do we do?

We grieve.

I'll bet that's not the answer you wanted. Doesn't sound exciting or heroic, does it?

Grief is not something we look forward to. We don't taste it and say, *"Yes! Give me more of that!"*

But grief is natural, common, and healthy.

Healthy?

Yes, healthy.

If we get injured and break the skin, we bleed. If we experience loss, our hearts get hit, and grief pours out.

Natural. Not easy. Frequently painful. But natural.

We will experience loss. If we care, we will grieve.

HOW WE GRIEVE MATTERS.

How we grieve matters. It's more important than any of us know. How we respond to loss and pain will shape our mindset and set the course for our lives.

In other words, how we grieve is huge.

I've experienced plenty of loss. For almost four decades now, my life has been about helping grieving people heal and grow. As a hospice chaplain and grief counselor, I'm around loss almost all the time. Grief is often the atmosphere I breathe.

In other words, this stuff is my specialty. Let me share with you some of the basics:

GARY'S 6 RULES OF HEALTHY GRIEVING

1. *Be kind to yourself.* Loss hurts.
2. *Be patient with yourself.* Recovery takes time.
3. *Get around people who love you and are helpful to you.* They will make a huge difference.
4. *Limit your exposure to people who aren't helpful to you.* You don't need extra drains right now.

5. *Express your grief well.* Talk, write, draw, paint, act, etc.
6. *Get out of your own head and intentionally serve others.* Serving those who can't give back to you is especially effective.

This isn't easy. Loss is tough. Grief is challenging. After every loss, life changes. After some losses, our entire world shakes. When we lose someone special to us, life will never be the same. We will never be the same.

This is why learning to grieve in healthy ways — including finding ways to use our losses for good — is a massively important life skill.

This is tough, but it can be done. You can do this.

CONSIDER:

Take a moment and think about the losses you've endured.

Here are some examples:

- Rejections
- Bullying
- Break-ups
- Disappointments
- Estrangements
- Failures
- Divorce
- Domestic violence
- Sexual abuse
- Moves
- Physical handicaps
- Serious illnesses
- Deaths

Make a list of your own losses. Write them down. Take your time. Chances are, there are a lot of them.

_____
_____
_____

Take a look at that list. Read through it out loud.
Close your eyes. Breathe deeply.
You're still here. You survived. That's huge.
You can do more than survive. You can thrive.
You can learn to use the painful stuff for good. You can make a difference in the way you respond to loss. Others will notice. You will inspire them. Difference-making is contagious.
If you sense any of these losses is affecting your life and heart in adverse ways and holding you back from growth and difference-making, let someone know. Share with someone you trust. Reach out. You'll be glad you did.

Look through your list of losses again. Choose one.
Can you think of ways you have grown and matured as a result of this loss?

_____
_____
_____

Can you think of ways you can use that loss for good in your own life and in the lives of others?

_____
_____
_____

Difference Makers find ways to turn losses into gains. Loss is painful. We need to grieve. And part of grieving well is turning things around and using those losses for good.

Life is full of loss. Let's use each one.

Difference Makers take loss seriously. They learn to grieve in healthy ways. They find ways to turn losses into gains.

IDEAS FOR EXPRESSING YOUR GRIEF:

- Talk out loud about what's going on inside you.
- Write your grief. Journal. Compose poetry, stories, or letters.
- Art your grief. Draw, paint, sculpt, act, woodwork, etc.
- Vent and share with trustworthy people.
- Find someone who knows grief well. Share, and then listen.
- Exercise regularly. This helps express grief more than you might guess.

CHAPTER 20
Anger

W E'VE TALKED ABOUT EMOTIONS. FEELINGS are real, but they are not necessarily reality. You can't afford to let how you feel at the moment control your mind and heart. Difference Makers learn to make decisions for the greater good, above and beyond what they might be feeling at the moment.

Speaking of emotions, anger is a common and powerful one. We all have reason to be angry from time to time.

Bad things happen. Much of life can seem unfair. All of us get blamed at some point for something we didn't do.

We have things taken from us. We lose opportunities, relationships, and people.

We ask, "Why?"

We get angry.

DEALING WITH ANGER

Difference Makers learn how to manage this powerful emotion. They accept the fact that they will have to deal with it on a regular basis.

The challenge is not so much the anger itself, but how it gets expressed, both by us and those around us. Difference Makers are aware of anger when it surfaces and find healthy and productive ways to release it.

Most of us try not to get angry. This sounds noble, but it's impossible. Anger-triggering words will be said. Angst-generating things will be done to us and to those we care about.

Also, it seems like we're living in an increasingly angry world. Anger in one person tends to illicit anger in another. Rage is contagious — and terrifying. Violent expressions of this powerful emotion can be terribly damaging and destructive. In anger's aftermath, lives can be dramatically altered, or even ended.

All of us have been on the receiving end of someone else's anger. We know what that feels like. Some of us have been the target of out-of-control rage. Still others of us have been victims of domestic violence and sexual abuse.

In some way, we've all been wounded by anger.

Though we might tend to think of anger as negative, it's actually neutral. The emotion itself is natural and even healthy in certain situations. It's the expression of the emotion that often gets us into trouble. Chances are, we've all wounded someone else with our anger.

Learning to manage this emotion is critical.

Imagine feeling angry and yet not taking it out on yourself or others.
Imagine being angry and also being able to
choose how you express and release it.
Imagine using anger to help yourself and others grow and heal.

Yes, it's possible. It can be done.
You can do it.

MANAGING THE ANGER THAT COMES.

First, know that nothing can come out of you except what's already in you. If you're angry, it came from inside. No one put it on you. Own the anger. Don't let it go underground and fester. You don't want that.

"*I feel angry.*"

Second, when the anger comes, pause. Count from 1 to 10, slowly. Focus on the numbers.

Third, breathe deeply. Picture yourself blowing the anger out.

Fourth, find a healthy way to express your anger.

What's a healthy expression of anger? One that doesn't harm you or others.

Here are some examples:

- Exercise. In a pinch, speed-walking while punching the air works great.
- Punch a pillow (or punching bag!).
- Scream (preferably when you're alone).
- Talk it out with someone you trust.
- Write it out in a journal, poem, song, or letter you will never send.
- Art it out (draw, paint, sculpt, etc.).

Again, deciding you'll never feel angry again won't work. Anger will come. You get bombarded on all sides, all the time. Good stuff. Bad stuff. In-between stuff. Your heart naturally reacts to all this. Anger is common and natural.

Difference Makers accept that anger will surface, and they own it when it does. Rather than lashing out, they pause, breathe, and find healthy ways to express what they're feeling. This is not easy in the heat of the moment, and sometimes Difference Makers fail. Then they smile and remember that they're not perfect. They're learning. They fail forward and chalk this episode up to experience.

You are a Difference Maker in training. Be patient with yourself. When you fail, fail forward.

CONSIDER:

Anger is common and natural. Finding healthy ways to express it is the challenge.

What typically triggers anger in you? When and in what situations do you find anger surfacing inside you? Take a moment and write some of these down.

_____

_____

_____

_____

_____

Now, read through your list and pick one that is especially challenging for you.

Imagine going into that situation and having your anger triggered.

See yourself counting from 1 to 10, focusing on the numbers.

See yourself breathing deeply. Picture yourself blowing the anger out.

Now see yourself expressing the anger in a healthy way.

If you want to, do the same process with another item on your list. And then another.

Visualizing these things is one way to be proactive and smart in handling this emotion.

Yes, you can actually plan beforehand how you're going to respond to difficult situations. No, things don't always go as planned, but that's okay. Like any other life skill, the more you practice it, the more a part of you it will become.

We all need good tools in our life toolbox. Good, healthy anger management is one of them.

And here's the really good news. *Whatever you learn, you can also pass along to others.* Some will notice the difference in how you handle your anger and seek you out.

Healthy emoting is attractive and magnetic. Difference Makers in training find themselves surrounded by others who want to be Difference Makers too.

> *Difference Makers don't let anger rule their hearts. They process it well and express it in healthy ways. Difference Makers learn to handle anger responsibly and use it for good.*

CHAPTER 21
Fear and Anxiety

I'll bet you can sense it. It seems to be everywhere.

It's fear.

We live in an increasingly fearful world. Most people try to fake it, putting on a tough exterior, but in reality, they're terrified.

Instead of becoming immobilized, you can learn to use fear for your own good and for the benefit of those around you. That's what Difference Makers do.

DEALING WITH FEAR AND ANXIETY

Fear leads to anxiety. This is an anxious, performance-oriented world. You will get anxious, but you can learn to overcome it. Difference Makers acknowledge that they feel anxious but let the truths they've internalized move them forward and out of Panic City.

Fear produces anxiety, and anxiety produces fear. They are interrelated — two sides of the same coin. The cycle they create can make a mess of things.

The answer is not telling yourself, *"I will not be afraid. I will not be anxious."* That won't work. This focuses your attention more on the fear and anxiety, which only makes matters worse.

You won't be able to keep fear or anxiety from coming. They're already here. They're all around you, all day, every day. They're practically in the air you breathe.

So, when these unwelcome visitors come knocking on your door, what do you do?

Breathe.
In through the nose. Out through the mouth.
Smell the roses. Blow out the candles.
Breathe. Slowly. Deeply.

When fear comes knocking, your brain thinks you're in danger. It triggers a fight-or-flight response. Then you *feel* like you're in danger, and the rest of your body begins to respond. If you don't step in and break this chain of events, anxiety often takes on a life of its own. It hijacks and immobilizes you. It takes over. Panic. Terror.

Eventually the panic passes. You're relieved. Then you feel embarrassed. Perhaps ashamed. Maybe defeated and worthless. The lies you've believed in the past come out of hiding and begin to flex their muscles.

The good news is that you can intervene. You can stop the fear-anxiety cycle quickly, before it picks up speed and spins out of control.

Breathe.
In through the nose. Out through the mouth.
Slowly. Deeply. Again, and again.

This puts the breaks on the fear-anxiety cycle by activating your parasympathetic nervous system. You're telling your brain, *"Slow down. It's okay. I'm okay."*

Your brain then sends signals to the rest of your body. *"It's not as bad as we thought. It's okay. We're okay."*

Trust me. It works.

The hard part is remembering to breathe when fear and anxiety hit. They ramp us up and cause us to either hold our breath or to breathe quick and shallow. Soon, we're visiting Panic City again.

Set your mind beforehand.

"Fear and anxiety will come knocking. When they do, I'll breathe."

Practice deep breathing when you're not anxious. Once a day at least. Make it a habit. Overall, you'll probably feel safer, more relaxed, and more focused. When trouble comes, our brains tend to respond the way they've been trained to. If deep breathing is already a habit, your brain will find that pathway quicker and initiate it sooner.

And here's another helpful thing to tell yourself when panic invades:

"It's not me. It's anxiety."

That anxiety — that panic — that's not you. It's an alien invader (even if it feels familiar). See it as something outside you.

Breathe.

Just breathe.

CONSIDER:

Fears. We all have them.

Think for a moment about yours. Make a list. Let it flow.

_____

_____

_____

Of the above, what are your top three fears? Number them. Most of our fears come from the lies buried deep inside us. Record your top three fears in order here:

1._____
2._____
3._____

What is the lie behind each one of them? Write these lies above next to the fear they correspond to.

Now, think of a corresponding truth that you can replace each of those lies with. Write these truths below:

1._____
2._____
3._____

On a scale of 1 to 10, with 10 being totally panicked, how would you rate your baseline anxiety (the amount of anxiety you normally live with on a daily basis)?

If you rate yourself at a 5 or higher, your system may have become used to living on hyper-alert. Your fight-or-flight mechanism gets activated easily.

If this describes where you're at, chances are you're going to need extra support to battle this obstacle and become more of the Difference Maker you were meant to be.

Who are you going to include in this to help support you (someone safe, whom you trust)?

Now, consider the following....

When or in what situations do you typically feel anxious? Think for a moment and make a list.

1._____
2._____
3._____

4._____
5._____

These are your typical anxiety triggers. It's good to be aware of them. Then, when you know you're going into one of these situations, you can actually prepare beforehand.

Let's practice.

You've been triggered. Anxiety comes at you.

Breathe.
Breathe deeply in through the nose and out through the mouth.
Smell the roses. Blow out the candles.
Again.
Say, "It's not me. It's anxiety."
Breathe.
Keep breathing.
Say, "Anxiety will come, and I'll be ready."
Breathe.
Again, the goal is not to never be anxious,
although that would be truly wonderful.
The goal is to manage anxiety better when it comes.

As you practice deep breathing and become more aware of your triggers, you will learn to deal with anxiety more quickly and effectively over time.

Remember:

"It's not me. It's anxiety."

Difference Makers aren't perfect. They never will be. They accept that anxiety will come knocking — many times forcefully. Sometimes they will manage it well, and sometimes they won't. They don't expect perfection of themselves. They rejoice in progress, even when it seems like it's three steps forward and two steps back.

Everyone's baseline anxiety level is different, but we all experience anxiety. Difference Makers learn to accept themselves where they are while moving forward. As a result, they visit Panic City less and less.

> *Anxiety and fear will come. Difference Makers know this. They learn to manage this challenging duo well and even use them for good.*

CHAPTER 22
Sadness, Depression, and Suicidal Thoughts

SADNESS IS A VALID HUMAN emotion. It's just not pleasant, so we don't like it.

We all feel sad sometimes. Maybe even a lot. Look at our world. There's a lot we could be sad about.

Intense sadness can lead to depression. Most of us have reason to feel depressed. Bad things happen. Our lives and screens are full of tragedy and trauma. Others of us struggle with neuro-chemical imbalances. Adversity is everywhere. Sadness, depression, and even hopelessness come knocking on our door daily.

Difference Makers accept these challenges and train themselves to climb these mountains, one step, one rock at a time.

Then there's apathy.

"Whatever."

We've all said it. Most of us think it more than we would like to admit.

If we don't succeed quickly, we give up. We live in Instant Land, where everything happens with the click of a mouse.

Difference Makers learn to tackle apathy rather than giving in to it. They don't run away from this listless form of adversity. They overcome it. You will too.

Most sadness, depression, and apathy are temporary. We experience a loss of some kind. Sadness is a natural and expected result. Feeling depressed is common during these times.

In our daily lives, feelings of sadness and even depression come, and then they go. When depression becomes persistent — when the intense sadness and lack of interest in life last for two weeks or more — it's time to reach out.

Seek out trustworthy people and share with them some of what you are going through. Stay open to their counsel and guidance.

There may even come a point where you wonder if life is worth it. If you're having thoughts of harming yourself, you need to tell someone immediately.

Who are you going to tell?
Spouse? Family member? Friend? Mentor? Physician? Counselor?
Suicide hotline (1-800-273-TALK)?
Crisis Text Line (text HOME to 741741)?
Decide now. Be prepared.

If you're currently having suicidal thoughts, **put this book down and reach out now.**

DEALING WITH SUICIDAL THOUGHTS

Suicide.

I encounter this subject a lot. Everyone seems to be talking about it. It's all over the news, social media, and in our entertainment.

It's almost as if suicide has become a fad. A trend. A meme.

Perhaps you'll remember from my own story that my mom attempted suicide shortly after my father died. You can imagine the thoughts that brought into my head.

"I'm not worth hanging around for."

"You're willing to make me an orphan. I obviously don't matter."

"There's no love here, or you wouldn't do this."

What was she thinking? I don't know. She never talked about what was happening inside her. I can only guess.

As a chaplain, over the last two years I've officiated at more than a dozen funerals of teens and others that took their own lives. As a grief counselor, I've followed some of these families and attempted to help them with the aftermath. The sadness, confusion, and anger are immense. The guilt is devastating. The ripple effects of suicide in the lives of parents, grandparents, siblings, and friends go on and on. Hearts are crushed and shattered. The impact is far from good. It's destructive. Those who take their own lives either knowingly or unknowingly thrust those who care about them into a suffocating cloud of pain.

Suicide is a forever decision that creates a plethora of devastation.

If you're having suicidal thoughts, or have struggled with them in the past, here are some things to remember...

Not every thought you have is yours. Some thoughts that run through your head don't originate with you. They came from others. They came from messages you've been fed and believed along the way.

We're all influenced by the thoughts, words, and actions of those around us. We're impacted by what we're exposed to (or expose ourselves to) in terms of media, literature, entertainment, relationships, etc.

In other words, if you're having thoughts of harming yourself or taking your own life, you're probably buying into messages you're getting from outside.

Are you going to let outside messages chart your course? Are you going to give your heart over to negative and destructive influences?

You can't afford to do that. You were designed for difference-making. The world needs you.

Suicidal thoughts ultimately come from lies.

If you tussle with suicidal thoughts, chances are you've swallowed some lies. Those lies are now exerting their influence.

"I'm a failure and a disappointment. I don't deserve to live."
"I have nothing to look forward to."
"The best is behind me. It's all downhill from here."
"It will always be this way."
"The pain is too great."
"I'm alone. No one cares."

All of these, and any version of them, ultimately come from a larger lie.

"Now is forever."

In other words, things won't get any better. Life will only get worse.

This lie then gives birth to another.

"There's no hope."

Then we personalize this.

"There's no hope for me."

The truth is that now is *not* forever. Things change. People change. You can change. Healing and growth are change, and you can do both.

Difference-making involves change, and you can do that too.

Hope is always here. The problem is our eyesight. If we have enough lies swirling around us, we can cease to recognize hope even if it's right under our own noses.

If hope seems to have departed, we need to somehow begin to blow away the dense fog that surrounds us so that we can see it again. Sometimes our vision is so off, and the pain is so great, that we have to search for hope. If we endure, we almost always find what we search for.

Hope is always with us. We just need eyes to see it. Most of the time, we need the help of others in this.

If you tend to believe that now is forever, begin replacing this lie with the truth.

"Now is not forever. I can heal and grow. Things can change."

If hope seems to have disappeared, and your mind is drifting toward believing that it no longer exists for you, replace that lie with the truth.

"Hope is always here. I will discover it over time."

Again, if you're having suicidal thoughts — or you tend to have them from time to time — that's an indication that you can't afford to go this alone any longer. Involve someone else in what you're thinking and feeling. Share with someone you trust. Get it out in the open.

When we share what's happening inside us, something happens. Pressure gets released. Another person now knows. Someone cares. There is hope. Things can change.

As long as you have self-destructive thoughts, keep sharing them. Find someone you can trust — or are willing to take the risk to trust — and share. Get it out. Keep getting it out. Lies have far more power when they are secret. When we hide, lies take on a life of their own apart from reality.

Yes, you might feel ashamed, embarrassed, or even frightened. You might even be terrified of sharing what you're thinking. That's natural.

Fear and shame, however, want to keep you stuck. They want to take over. They want to keep you locked in the cycle of secret thoughts.

You are not the fear you feel. You are not the shame you experience. Fear and shame are barriers to healing, growth, and difference-making.

Share. When you're real with someone else about what's going on inside you, you open yourself up to good things.

CONSIDER:

Chances are you've had your share of sadness and depression.

Think for a moment. *When do you tend to feel sad or depressed? What seems to trigger these emotions for you?* List a few of them here.

1._____

2._____

3._____

Some sad and depressed feelings are the result of loss or disappointment. Is that the case with any of the scenarios on your list above?

_____

_____

_____

Look over your list again. Can you see any lies exerting their influence in these times of sadness or depression? If so, write them down.

_____

_____

_____

Now, see if you can craft a truth from each of the lies you wrote above.

_____

_____

_____

Difference Makers set their minds on truth. Most lies are deep rooted. They're used to us giving them our allegiance. When we turn away from them toward the truth, these lies get noisy. They scream for attention and make themselves a real nuisance.

Keep setting your mind on the truth. As you tune your heart to truth's voice, the lies of the past will eventually become static in the background.

Yes, you can learn to do this.

As you tell yourself the truth about you and begin to live like it's true, over time, you will heal and grow. Less burdened by debilitating lies, you'll live more in freedom and with a greater sense of mission and purpose.

Difference Makers accept some sadness and depression as part of life, but they learn to manage these emotions. You will too.

> *Difference Makers know that sadness and depression will come. They learn to manage these emotions, and then use them for good.*

WHERE WE'VE BEEN AND WHERE WE'RE GOING

You've been on quite a journey already.

We've talked about how lies infiltrate our lives and influence our hearts and minds more than we realize. *Difference Makers expose the lies they've believed and become vigilant against them.*

We've discovered things that are true about all of us – true about you. *Difference Makers embrace the truth about themselves and use it to propel them forward.* They remain on guard against lies and intentionally replace them with the truth.

In this section, we've talked about some of the obstacles that Difference Makers face along the way.

We encounter loss. We experience little deaths, big deaths, and other bad things. It's not so much what happens, but how you interpret and respond to what happens that makes all the difference. *Difference Makers learn to grieve well and use loss, pain, and hardship for good.*

We encounter anger – in ourselves and in others. Managing this powerful emotion well can be a challenge. *Difference Makers learn to acknowledge anger quickly and then express it in healthy ways.*

We encounter fear and anxiety. They can threaten to derail you – your life, health, and relationships. *Difference Makers understand that fear and anxiety will come knocking. They learn to acknowledge them and then release them (over, and over again, if necessary).*

We encounter sadness, depression, and even self-destructive thoughts. Most sadness and depression are situational and temporary. When they linger, self-harming and suicidal thoughts can begin to emerge. *Difference Makers are aware of this and involve someone else quickly when these invaders approach.*

You're designed for connection. There may be times you want to isolate, but that's the last thing you should do. Remember how unique, valuable, and significant you are. When you're hurting, reach out.

In the next section, we're going to talk about discovering who you are and why you're here. *Difference Makers are passionate about their mission.* They know they're here for a reason.

You have a unique role to play and a personal mission to fulfill. It's time to discover it.

Difference Makers don't expect life to be a smooth superhighway.
They know life is a rocky and challenging path.
Difference Makers expect obstacles and learn to deal with them.
Problems will come.
We will deal with them honestly and responsibly.
We will live from our hearts and respect those around us.
We hurdle obstacles and overcome adversity.
We are Difference Makers.

PART FIVE
LAUNCHING YOU ON YOUR MISSION!
(Discovering Why You're Here and How to Live Your Purpose)

WHEN I WAS A COLLEGE student, a mentor of mine said something that would become a guiding beacon for me in life.

"*Give someone a big enough 'why' and they can endure any 'what.'*"

He was talking about mission.

If a person doesn't know why they're here, they're destined to make life about themselves. Small living without any driving purpose is the overall result.

Who are you? Why are you here? Do you know?

Frankly, most people don't.

No wonder we wander through life angry and frustrated. We're moving, but where are we going?

Difference Makers have a rock-solid, well-defined mission. They know why they're here and what they're about. Their mission launches them out of bed each day and into a world thirsting for their contribution. Difference Makers live purpose-driven, mission-oriented lives.

The goal of this section is to help you discover and define your mission. We'll talk about Mission Busters and Mission Builders, and how to avoid the former and develop the latter. And hopefully, when we're done, you'll launch yourself on a clearer path than you've ever had before.

You'll be on your way to becoming the Difference Maker you were designed to be.

CHAPTER 23
MISSION CRISIS!

WE ARE IN A CRISIS. We lack mission. Most people live too small. Honestly, most have no defined mission that they can articulate. Many end up throttled by winds of change that blow through their lives. They're upended by loss, disappointment, and the death of dreams.

An amazing number of people rise from their pillows each morning and go through the motions, doing what they need to do to get what they think their needs are met. They're on a treadmill going nowhere.

In other words, they're moving and working, but they have no shining light to guide them. Their purpose isn't big enough. They have no mission larger than themselves.

WHAT WE DO AND WHO WE ARE

Our lack of mission is revealed by how we introduce ourselves to others. We tend to mention our name and then tell people what we *do*.

We learn this early.

"I'm a student."

"I'm a football player."

"I'm a future model."

Once we get into a job or career, this gets cemented further.

"I'm a nurse." "I'm a mother." "I'm an accountant." "I'm a mechanic." "I'm an attorney." And so on.

"*I am a _____,*" is a statement of identity. We're defining ourselves by what we do — our work. But our work is not who we are. We are more than our jobs. Our vocations are roles that we play, but they are not who we are.

You might be a successful attorney, but then something happens, and you lose your license to practice law. The same could be true for a nurse, doctor, counselor, or any other licensed vocation.

You could give your life to a company and define your existence by your job. One day the company might go under or be bought out. You could be terminated or laid off. If that company was your mission, you now have to find another one.

You might be a financial adviser and after a decade get burned out and have to move on to something else. Currently, the average person will change not merely jobs but careers three to five times during their working life.

Clearly, we are not what we do. Not even close.

There are other roles we play in life, such as our position in our families.

Daughter, son, sister, brother, niece, nephew, cousin, aunt, uncle, grandchild, mother, father, grandparent. These are all roles, and extremely important ones. They shape who we are and who we become.

But even these roles, though tied closely to our identities, are not, strictly speaking, who we are.

Family roles too can be stripped away from us. Tragedies can happen, and suddenly we are no longer a grandchild, child, or parent.

Anything that we can lose is not our identity. We are not what we do. We are not our position in our families.

Our mission — why we are here — must be large enough to include all our roles in life and yet supersede them all.

Our mission must be large enough to endure upset, loss, pain, illness, and anything else that could potentially assault it.

No wonder we're in a mission crisis.

We don't know who we are or why we're here. We wander. We bounce. We play disposable careers, relationships, and families. We are driven along by the daily grind of trying to survive, and then trying to succeed, and then trying to succeed more, all with the goal of having perfect families and marriages along the way and finally retiring in some exotic spot where we can "get away from it all."

No. You were made for more than this.

You were made to be a Difference Maker. You were designed for impact. Meaning oozes from your pores.

Don't get bogged down in the current worldwide mission crisis. Rise above it.

Commit yourself to discover your mission, and then live it.

You'll be glad you did.

CONSIDER:

Think for a moment about some of the roles you have in life. Son, daughter, mom, dad, employee, supervisor, boss, grandparent, etc.

List your roles. Try to get them all down - everything you can think of.

_____

_____

_____

Look at your list. If you could rank them, which ones would be in your top five? Mark them.

If you lost these roles, how different would your life be?

_____

_____

_____

Losing some or perhaps any of these could be crushing. It might be so devastating you could wonder who you are now.

Loss can have massive impact, but it does not determine who you are.

Can you look at this list and see that these are all roles you occupy, but they are not your identity? In other words, can you see that you are more than any and all roles you can have in life?

Can you see that your mission, whatever it is, must be large enough to include all these roles and yet be above and beyond them all?

If you had to say what your mission is right now, what would it be?

_____

_____

_____

We are in a mission crisis. Difference Makers see this and pursue even greater clarity about who they are and why they're here.

CHAPTER 24
MISSION DEFINED

As we said in the previous chapter, our personal missions must be big enough to include all the roles we play in life and still be beyond them all. Our mission must be strong and large enough to weather all storms, trouble, tragedies, and attacks. Our *why* must be big enough to endure any *what*.

So, what is it? Why are we here? What's our mission? What's yours?

WHATEVER YOUR MISSION IS, IT MUST FLOW FROM YOUR HEART.

Your heart is your most prized possession and the guts of who you are. Everything in your life flows from it.

Most of us walk through life silencing our hearts. We get hurt and wounded. We pull back and begin to live life playing defense. We buy into the lies, put on our emotional hoodies, and hide. We develop the art of mask-wearing. Our hearts go underground.

We long to be known, but we're frightened. After a while, we might even forget who we are. We become what we perceive others want to see. We're performers on a stage, while our hearts scream for attention from some forgotten place deep inside us.

No more. You must find your heart.

Once you find it, you must live from it.

Whatever your mission is, it must flow from your heart.

WHATEVER YOU MISSION IS, IT INCLUDES OTHER PEOPLE.

You came out of the womb needing and seeking relationship. You've been at it ever since. Life is about relationships, and so your mission will be too.

You might be an introvert. You might be an extrovert. It doesn't matter. Some have many relationships. Some have few. Some relationships are shallow. Others are deep.

Whether you're rolling in friends or have just a couple, your mission will include and be about other people. We're in this together. When we live only for ourselves, life becomes painful and small. Relationships are challenging, but they are the spice of life.

Your mission, whatever it is, will include people and relationships.

WHATEVER YOUR MISSION IS, IT MUST BE MOTIVATED BY LOVE.

What kind of love are we talking about here?

We're talking about the kind of love that is willing to enter another person's world, accept them for who they are, and act for their good.

We all long to be loved like this — unconditionally. We yearn to be embraced where we are, as we are, even with all our messes and failures. You've been seeking this love since you were born. We all have. You've experienced it from time to time. It felt so safe, secure, and powerful.

The love we all long for, in its purest form, is a gift. It gives and expects nothing in return. It delights in the giving, and that's enough. The irony is that the one who loves expecting nothing in return ends up receiving love back again — somehow, some way.

Let's think about this again, for it seems almost too good to be true.

Love gives. And gives. It gives freely, with no strings attached.

In the process of giving without the expectation of getting, love somehow returns to the one who gives it.

This love is your calling. It's mine too. We won't get it perfect, but we can pursue it. We can grow in learning to love with fewer expectations and strings attached. Every little bit counts.

Whatever your mission is, it will include learning to love freely and sacrificially. Your heart longs to do this, even if you're not aware of it. Nothing fulfills like love freely given.

WHATEVER YOUR MISSION IS, IT WILL BE ABOUT SERVICE.

If your mission comes from your heart, includes people and relationships, and is fundamentally about learning to love freely and unconditionally, it makes sense that your mission — whatever it is — will be about service.

Service to others for their good.
Service to your community for its good.
Service to the world for the greater good.

Service is love in action. We intentionally get out of our own heads and reach out to others. We seek to use our gifts, talents, and abilities for the benefit of others. We change our mindset from *me* to *we*.

Service is a mysterious thing. It exercises the heart in ways that lead to greater mental, emotional, spiritual, and even physical health. As we serve, our hearts begin to come alive. We see others more. We live more in the present. We are less burdened by our own, private stuff. Life takes on greater meaning. We live larger than ever before.

Here is the basic truth about service that I've seen in my own life and in the lives of countless others:

As we serve, we become more of who we were designed to be, and what we need tends to come back to us in extraordinary ways.
We receive as we give.
We heal as we serve.
We grow as we live for the greater good.
And over time, we become more of the Difference Makers we really are.

WE'RE IN THIS TOGETHER. WE'RE WIRED TO SERVE.

The more we engage in service, the more fulfilled we will be. The more we deny or neglect our calling to serve, the smaller our lives become and the more we will struggle inside.

You are already a Difference Maker. What kind of difference and how much is yet to be seen.

In review, whatever your mission is, it will...

- Flow from your heart.
- Be about people and relationships.
- Be about learning to love freely and unconditionally.
- Be about service.

Again, the four key words that drive your mission are:

Heart.
People.
Love.
Service.

You might be thinking, *"Impossible. You don't know me and my situation."*

You're right. I don't.

But I do know some things about you.

You are human.

You have a heart.

You are wired for relationship, whether you're an introvert or extrovert.

You need love, and your heart wants to give it.

You are far from alone. We're in this together. Your mission is bigger than you are. You're here to serve and make an impact for the greater good.

You are a Difference Maker.

CONSIDER:

Heart. People. Love. Service.

Let's think about these for a moment.

HEART

How do you see your own heart? What words would you use to describe who you are inside? Take a moment and make a list.

_____

_____

_____

Looking at the above list, are there any words you wish weren't there? Any words you wish were?

_____

_____

_____

If you could redefine your heart, what would you want it to be like? Be as descriptive as possible.

_____

_____

_____

Honestly, many of us don't know our own hearts very well. The heart is mysterious. It is molded and shaped by life, experience, and the people around us.

This is good news. It means that you're not stuck. You can make decisions along the way that move your heart to where you want it to be.

Every heart wants love. Every heart wants to love. Every heart is wired for connection. That's why these four words go together: Heart, People, Love, Service.

PEOPLE

Think again about what kind of heart you want to pursue. Who do you know has a heart like that? List them here.

_____

_____

_____

You are shaped and influenced greatly by the people you're around the most. Are you spending time with people who have hearts you admire and want to emulate?

Are there some negative influences or people in your life? How much are you affected by them? Do you need to limit your time with them or your exposure to them?

Hearts long to be seen and heard. If we give what others need, we usually get back what we need. In other words, as you see others and take time to hear them, that gift will return to you.

What would it mean for you to *see* the people around you? Think about family, friends, and co-workers. List some names here.

_____

_____

_____

What would it mean to *see* and *hear* these people?

_____

_____

_____

Think about some people you encounter that might be *invisible* to many of those around them. Take some time. Make a list.

_____

_____

_____

What would it mean to *see* and *hear* these people whom you probably don't know? Write down some ideas.

_____

_____

_____

LOVE

Think about the people you listed in the previous section. How can you *love* them?

Love begins with seeing and hearing someone. That's huge.

Another biggie is *affirmation.*

Affirmation is when you see something you like or admire, and you tell them. It can be as simple as a sincere thank you.

Look at your list of family and friends. Think about how you might affirm them. Take a moment and brainstorm. Write their name again, and then how you can affirm them.

_____

_____

_____

Look at your list of often-invisible people. How can you affirm them? How can you say thank you in a way that's meaningful?

Invisible people have names. Most of them have name badges. Try noticing their name and greeting them warmly. When you use their name, watch their reaction.

Then affirm them somehow. Thank them for the job they are doing.

How will you affirm some of these often-invisible people in the days ahead?

_____

_____

_____

SERVICE

When you think of service, what comes to mind?

_____

_____

_____

Can you think of a few ways you can serve family and friends?

_____

_____

_____

When you hear the phrase *"serve for the greater good,"* what comes to mind? Can you list some examples?

_____

_____

_____

How might *you* serve the greater good (including people you don't know)? Can you list some possibilities?

_____

_____

_____

HEART. PEOPLE. LOVE. SERVICE.

Put these together, and you get Difference Makers who are living out their mission. As they live from their heart, see the people around them, learn to love, and engage in service for the greater good, the ripple effects multiply. Everything counts. Little things become huge in the end.

Take the small steps today. And again tomorrow. After a month, you'll be surprised how far down the road of impact you have gone. And after a year, who knows?

Develop the habits of difference-making. Exercise your heart. See people. Learn to act for the good of the other person. Serve for the greater good.

And look out.

Difference Makers train themselves to see people and then serve them. They learn to think, speak, and act for the greater good.

CHAPTER 25
MISSION BUSTERS

In the previous chapter, we talked about defining your mission. Difference Makers' missions revolve around four things: Heart, People, Love, and Service.

In the fight to become the Difference Maker you were made to be, there are things that will help you in this battle and things that won't. There are Mission Builders and there are Mission Busters. In this chapter, we'll tackle the things that trip you up on your difference-making journey, or even scuttle it altogether.

MISSION BUSTER #1: SELF-OBSESSION

Of course, if we're going to be Difference Makers for good, we have to get out of our own heads. Frankly, however, our world doesn't help much with this.

We live in the age of selfies. Our cameras always seem to be focused on us, and we are the ones pointing them. Here's me, how I look, what I'm doing, and what's happening with me.

Me. Me. Me.

If we look at the world as a whole, it certainly seems like human beings are naturally prone to selfishness. We're out to get our needs met – what we think our needs are — no matter what it takes.

No wonder we struggle with loneliness. We set ourselves up for it.

Self-focus is a lose-lose scenario. In our desperation to be seen and loved, we cease to see and love. We make everything about ourselves. What *we* think. How *we* feel. What *we* want.

Our hearts shrink. Our mission is not lived. Others are not seen and loved by us.

Self-focus is an easy road that leads to the destruction of your heart.

Difference Makers walk a different path. They have discovered that self-focus is a dead-end road where all you're left with is, well, yourself. Difference Makers know selfishness will bust not only their own life and mission but will wound others too.

MISSION BUSTER #2: ARROGANCE

Every heart is tempted toward arrogance. We confuse significance with power. We buy into the lie that being on top means being better or more valuable.

> *"It's a dog-eat-dog world."*
> *"I'm looking out for number one."*
> *"I'm nobody's doormat."*

Somewhere deep inside, we feel threatened. The world is out to get us. People are out to get us. We must protect ourselves. We reason the best way to protect ourselves is to make ourselves invincible. Knocking down other people and crawling over them becomes a success strategy.

Our hearts harden. When we meet another person, we don't see a unique and valuable individual. We see competition.

The ultimate arrogance is the refusal to become the Difference Makers we are capable of being and saying instead, "This is *my* life. I will do what I want, when I want."

None of us chose to be born. None of us chose who we were going to be born to or where. None of us causes our own heart to beat. How can this be *my* life or *your* life?

Yes, we are individuals, but we are in this together. It's *we*, not *me*.

Arrogance is the fuel behind self-focused living. And in turn, self-focus fuels more arrogance.

Difference Makers recognize the danger of arrogance. They know it will ultimately destroy their heart and derail their mission.

MISSION BUSTER #3: COMPARISON

We come out of the womb and almost immediately try to discover who we are. The world around us sends messages that enter our hearts and take root. Early on, we learn the strategy of looking around us, sizing things up, and trying to figure out our place in the world.

As we grow, other messages hit us. What's good? What's beautiful? What's attractive, successful, and valuable?

Then we look in the mirror. We compare. How do we stack up?

By the time we hit elementary school, comparison is already a well-developed, deeply-rooted mental habit.

Looks. Clothes. Money. Cars. Houses. Talents. Intelligence.

We'll compare anything, anywhere, anytime, with anybody.

Again, most of this isn't intentional. It's habit. We've learned to compare. It's ingrained in us.

Here's the good news. If we learned to do it, we can learn to not do it. Or at least, we can learn to do something else in its place.

Difference Makers are aware of their tendency to compare and compete. In sports and other things, competing against others is part of the game. In the game of life, Difference Makers learn to compete *for* others rather than *against* them.

Comparison is a thief that robs hearts of joy and contentment. When we compare, we lose.

MISSION BUSTER #4: DECEPTION

We're born seeking connection. Life is about relationships.

Deception, therefore, works against the core of who we are and why we're here.

Yes, we all wear masks. We pose and posture. We spin things. We try on some level to control situations and other people to get what we want. We manipulate.

We've also been wounded. We protect ourselves. We hide. We shade the truth.

Many times, we lie. White lies maybe, but lies nonetheless.

In *Hamlet*, Shakespeare said it this way:

"God hath given you one face and you make yourselves another."

Yes, deception runs deep in us. No one is perfect. No one is perfectly honest. Habitual deception on the other hand, hurts others and destroys relationships.

Lying strangles the heart over time. Life becomes a lie.

Difference Makers are aware of the human propensity for mask-wearing. As they mature, they seek to discover their masks, and get rid of them one by one. They begin to notice when they are posturing, spinning, and attempting to present themselves as better than they are.

Difference Makers seek to live honestly. They want to be truthful, and therefore, trustworthy.

MISSION BUSTER #5: GOSSIP

Words pack power. More than we realize.

Gossip is saying something about a person who is not present in such a way that it can dishonor them.

Gossip is cowardly. The person is not there to defend themselves or to hold us accountable.

Honestly, we've all engaged in gossip on some level. Before we even realize it, conversations drift that direction. It's like we don't know how to share our own hearts or speak positively about others. And no wonder. We're surrounded by negative messages and half-truths.

Difference Makers know the danger of gossip. They also know that one who habitually gossips is not their friend.

If they'll say it to you, they'll say it about you. The Gossip knows no secrets and no confidences. They are seeking attention (and ultimately love) by bringing others down.

Gossip poisons the heart. It wounds people. It shatters relationships. And ultimately, it destroys the character of the one who engages in it.

Difference Makers know the definition of gossip and are on guard against it. They avoid it like the plague. When someone around them engages in gossip, Difference Makers politely excuse themselves and walk away. Other more confrontational Difference Makers might hold the speaker accountable, saying something like, *"That person isn't here right now, so let's talk about something else."*

Difference Makers protect their own hearts. When they can, they also protect the reputation of others. They see gossip for what it is — an enemy of their hearts.

MISSION BUSTER #6: GREED / ENVY

When we compare, sooner or later we find ourselves battling with envy. We're jealous. We wish we were someone one. We wish we had this or that.

We look on social media. Everyone's perfect. Carefully posed selfies. Filters. Blemishes removed. Augmentations made. Perfect.

Everyone else has it good. Clothes. Cars. Houses. Possessions. Opportunities. Romantic attachments. Happy marriages. Wonderful families. Amazing relationships. Everybody is smiling and happy.

Envy is familiar to us. It comes naturally with comparison, and we've been comparing and competing for a long time.

Envy separates people. It distances us from others.

Then there's the driving force behind envy: Greed.

We want more. More of this. More of that.

Sometimes we get what we want. It doesn't satisfy. We want more.

When we look to the world and others to define us, we always come up short. We never seem to arrive. We chase looks, possessions, status, happiness, and power in the blind dash to feel better.

Yet, we always seem to be disappointed in the end.

We're insatiable.

Greed seems to be a universal human condition.

Difference Makers understand that they're prone to greed and envy, but they also know this ugly duo is terribly destructive. Difference Makers are on the watch for greed because it is an enemy of their hearts, relationships, and missions.

MISSION BUSTER #7: BITTERNESS / HATRED

We've all been wounded. We're all prone to comparison. Jealousy, envy, and greed grow easily in the soil of our minds and hearts. If left unchecked, bitterness can grow, and hatred can follow.

Bitterness and hatred are the summit of the self-focused life. We stifle our hearts and squarely place the blame for who we are and where we are on other people. Anger takes over and drives our existence.

We see examples of this everywhere in our world. If you look hard enough, you can see it in your own life too. None of us are immune to bitterness and hatred. Once they take root, they tend to grow quickly, like a weed.

If bitterness resides in a heart, it seeps out and affects all that person's relationships. Yes, all of them and not just the one they are in conflict with. Hatred becomes a cancer that weaves its way into every part of life.

Difference Makers know the danger of bitterness. They work hard to keep the tentacles of offenses, hurts, and rejections from gripping them too tightly. They seek to deal responsibly with their pain, including that which has been shoved on them by others.

Difference Makers are aware of what bitterness and hatred have produced in human history, and they want no part in that.

MISSIONS BUSTER #8: REVENGE

Pay back. Do to others as they have done to you. If someone hurts us or someone we care about, we strike back.

Revenge is the result, on some level, of anger that spawned bitterness that in turn led to hatred. We grimace and plot. We will make the culprits pay for what they have done.

There is a difference, of course, between justice and revenge. Justice is out of our hands in many ways, though we all tend to reap what we sow. In many cases, justice does come to the guilty, and we can play a part in that.

Revenge, on the other hand, is taking matters into our own hands. This never works out well. The results are never fully satisfying. Whatever revenge we manage to exact can't replace what or who was taken or take away the results of what happened. And afterwards, we're left with our own hearts. We've played the game of the one we're trying to get back at. We've fought fire with fire, and now there's nothing left. We've reduced ourselves to the level of the one who wronged us. We've traded our hearts for theirs.

Difference Makers flee revenge thinking. They know it profits no one, especially themselves and those they care about. They refuse to let evil or any of its manifestations derail or distract them from their missions.

Difference Makers don't stoop down to revenge, but rather rise above it to something much greater.

AN UGLY LIST

It's an ugly list, isn't it?

Self-focused selfishness.
Arrogance.
Comparison.

Deception.
Envy and greed.
Bitterness and hatred.
Revenge.

We all struggle with these things, but they are enemies of the Difference Maker's heart. They will derail you and your mission. They are life-busters.

See them for the folly that they are. Learn to recognize them in yourself.

This is a battle.

No matter how entrenched any of these might be in your life, you can overcome them. We battle these enemies by replacing them with friends. We trade Mission Busters for Mission Builders.

What are Mission Builders?

More on that in the next chapter.

CONSIDER:

This could be tough exercise, but it will be well worth it. Consider the Mission Buster list again:

Self-focused selfishness
Arrogance
Comparison
Deception
Envy and greed
Bitterness and hatred
Revenge

Can you see how all these relate? One leads to another, and so on. They are like a web, and as the strand of one Buster takes hold and thickens, it strengthens the entire Buster system. All the Mission Busters weave in and out of each other all the time.

In your Mission Buster web, which strand is the thickest? Which one seems to pop out at you and say, *"Yeah, I do this a lot"?*

MY #1 MISSION BUSTER:

Take a moment and write down how you see this Buster operating in your heart and life. Be as specific as you can.

Where I can see this Mission Buster in my life:

_____

_____

_____

Next, pick another Buster that is messing with your life. Do the same thing. Write down how this enemy of your heart is showing itself. Again, be specific.

MY #2 MISSION BUSTER:

How I see this Mission Buster showing itself in my life:

_____

_____

_____

You might get overwhelmed and say, *"Ack! The whole list is me! I'm done for!"*

No, these Busters are not you. You struggle with them, but they are not who you are.

You are a Difference Maker.

Difference Makers are aware of this nasty web of Busters, but they don't focus on it. They don't spend time and energy trying to kick these ugly intruders out the door. Difference Makers focus on the good. Instead of staring at the glaring negatives, they choose to gaze at the potential positives.

Difference Makers focus their attention on Mission Builders.

As we plant Mission Builders in our lives, their roots begin to crowd out the Mission Busters. Pursue the good, and the other stuff will recede into your rearview mirror.

What are Mission Builders and what might they mean for you? Read on.

Difference Makers are aware of Mission Busters so they can effectively deal with them when they surface. Difference Makers are on guard against things that endanger their hearts.

CHAPTER 26
MISSION BUILDERS

You have a toolbox. You're building something. Something great.

It's your life.

To build well, you're going to need some good, dependable tools.

Heart. People. Love. Service. These are the foci of the Difference Maker. You are building a remarkable life of impact for good.

If that's what you're building, what kind of tools do you need?

You need Mission Builders.

MISSION BUILDER #1: OBSERVATION

Difference Makers see what and who is around them. They notice things and people. Perhaps the largest and first benefit of getting out of our own heads is discovering that there is a world out there that doesn't revolve around us.

It's amazing what can happen when we put down our screens and take note of what's around us. Nature. Clouds. Birds. Animals. Colors. Shapes. People.

And oh, the people. What variety! Skin. Eyes. Shapes. Hair. Faces.

Many choose to immerse themselves in a personal tech world rather than the real one directly in front of them. Frankly, there's plenty of time for both. When we choose screen over flesh and blood, especially at the family dinner table, in public places, sporting events, etc., we slowly train ourselves to live in a digital world that we can manipulate and surf. We're used to hiding — and we're good at it. If we're not careful, our tech can be one more way to retreat away from the reality of the relationships and people around us.

I'm not a techy, but I slipped into the habit of looking at my phone with every blip, ping, bong, and ring. I didn't like the results.

I now have a time of media-fasting every day. This is a block of time where I put all screens aside and engage with the world immediately around me. I've been doing this several months now, and I'm much richer for it. My heart is less hurried, less distracted, and more focused on people and my immediate reality.

If we want good relationships, we must become better observers. If we want to love and be loved, we need hearts and minds undistracted enough to notice people.

Difference Makers embrace the wisdom of Sir Arthur Conan Doyle's character Sherlock Holmes. When asked by his sidekick Dr. Watson why he can't seem to get what Sherlock does from any given situation, the famous private detective replies:

> *"You see, but you do not observe."*

Difference Makers learn to observe. They put distractions aside and begin to see this amazing world and the people in it. They know they're a part something bigger. Their hearts expand.

MISSION BUILDER #2: HUMILITY

Someone once described humility as *right-sizing yourself.*

We wrestle with finding out who we are and our place in this world. Amid the conflicting messages and personal comparisons, we tend to pendulum swing back and forth from the extremes of *up-sizing* and *down-sizing* ourselves. We typically see ourselves as better or worse than the reality, and rarely as we truly are.

Perhaps as humans the ability to see ourselves as we are is beyond us. Certainly, we don't see ourselves perfectly. The goal is to come as close as possible to the truth.

Valuable. Imperfect. Lovable. Significant.

As we see the lies we've believed and begin to replace them with the truth, our view of ourselves changes. As we hold the truth about us in balance, humility emerges.

We right-size ourselves.

The world is not about us but needs us. Life is not about us but includes us. We are not all-important, but we can each make a massive difference.

Humility is not becoming a doormat. Humility is not becoming silent when the good demands we speak out. Humility is not shyness or timidity. Humility is owning up to who we are — no more, no less.

Difference Makers are passionate about learning to see themselves accurately. This is the key to being able to live confidently in truth. They stop looking around them for meaning, and discover it in the simple four-word phrase: *Heart-People-Love-Service.* Difference Makers want to simply be themselves, and become more of who they are with each passing day.

Life is not about you, but it includes you.

The universe is not about you, but you are a crucial part of it.

You don't control people or situations, but you have more influence than you realize.

You were meant to live from your heart, in love and service to others. As you do this, you'll discover more and more about yourself, the world, and people.

MISSION BUILDER #3: SELF-ACCEPTANCE

Difference Makers learn to accept themselves where they are, as they are.

This is not complacency. This is not laziness or lack of

responsibility. Difference Makers are interested in healing, growth, and impact. In order to live well, they have to be honest about themselves and accept where they are at present.

If I'm in New York and want to go to Hawaii, I could wish that I was already on a plane and over the Pacific, but that wouldn't be reality. The wishing doesn't get me any nearer the islands. Accepting that I'm a long way from Hawaii, on the other hand, can help me make plans to eventually get there. The right plans can get me closer to that long plane ride.

Difference Makers accept where they are, but they don't expect to stay there. They expect to progress, heal, grow, and make a positive difference in others' lives.

Many, however, opt for one of the following:

"I'll never get there. Difference-making is too far away for me."

"I'm perfect. I don't need to change anything. It's other people who need to change."

Both of these statements come from people who have not accepted themselves as they are where they are. Both live in realities of their own making that have been shaped by lies and limiting beliefs. One has given up. The other thinks they don't need to try. The end result for both is the same.

Stuck-ness.

Accept yourself as you are. You need this from yourself.

But don't stay where you are. Stand up. Move forward. Choose to learn, heal, and grow. Develop your heart and live from it.

You're on the right road. Difference-making is straight ahead.

MISSION BUILDER #4: LISTENING

Listening appears to be a lost art.

Same old story. Everyone wants to be heard. No one wants to listen.

Listening is work. It means putting aside your own agenda and focusing on the other person.

It means being willing to show up and be quiet.

It means hearing their words but listening for their heart.

It means asking good questions to make sure you understand what they're saying.

It even might mean repeating back to them what you hear to make sure you get it. Otherwise, you — and they — have no way of knowing whether you really understood or not.

Listening means entering another person's world and being with them there, even if it's only for a little while.

Honestly, few of us listen. Most of us are waiting until someone finishes talking so we can respond. Of course, that's all about us. In that scenario, we don't know whether we've understood them or not. And worse yet, their hearts go unseen and unheard. On some level, they know you're not really with them.

You've been on the receiving end of this kind of non-listening plenty of times. You know how it feels.

It's time for a change.

Your heart wants to listen. It wants to love. It wants to reach out and make the difference needed in that moment.

You can learn to listen. It might feel like an uphill battle. That's okay. Be patient with yourself. Celebrate each little success.

Difference Makers must revive the lost art of listening and make it a central part of their skill set.

The world will thank you. You'll thank yourself too.

MISSION BUILDER #5: GENUINE INTEREST

In order to make a difference, you have to actually care.

People are smart. They know whether your interest is genuine. Most people can smell a fake a mile away.

If you're hard on yourself, you might wonder sometimes if you actually do care. The truth about all of us is sometimes we do, sometimes we don't, and everything in between.

No matter where you are on this care spectrum, here's the good news:

> *If you grow in and develop the Mission*
> *Builders we've talked about so far –*
> *observation, humility, self-acceptance, and listening –*
> *you <u>will</u> genuinely care.*
> *You won't be able not to.*

How do I know this?

Because people are fascinating, that's why. Even the people who bore you and those you can't stand. They're interesting. We all are.

Once you detach a little from making it all about you, you'll become freer to let it be about the person in front of you. You don't have to do anything, figure out anything, or fix anything. You're just there.

You put all else aside. You observe. You listen.

People will surprise you. They're fascinating. Each one unique, valuable, and imperfect. Each person wrestling to figure themselves, others, and life out. Everybody posturing and looking for acceptance, love, and purpose.

> *Put aside your normal likes and dislikes.*
> *Be quiet. Observe. Listen.*
> *Do this, and you can't help but be genuinely interested.*

Their hearts will sense your genuineness. And boom. You're on your way to difference-making with them.

MISSION BUILDER #6: HONESTY / AUTHENTICITY

In order to make a difference for good, honesty must be part of your toolset.

Most people think of honesty as telling the truth. That's certainly part of it, but honesty is more than this. It goes beyond words. It comes from the heart.

Most of us desire to be ourselves in such a way as to benefit others. We're designed for this. We get tripped up by comparison, gossip, envy, and pettiness. We end up hiding. Most of us have mastered how to manipulate and deceive to get what we want. These things are honesty killers.

Be honest with yourself. Begin to be more honest with others.

Hide less. Express your heart more.

Find a few trustworthy people you can be real with. You need people with whom you can share what's going on inside you without fear of judgment. Get around safe people who inspire you and who listen well.

If you want to be honest, get around honest people. Rub shoulders with those who live out who they are in service to others.

Honest people know how to hold their tongues. What comes out of their mouths will be true. Yet not everything that's true will come out of their mouths. Some things might be true, but it might not be loving in the moment to say that. Wise, honest people know the difference because they've practiced this balance of tongue-holding and truth-telling over time.

If it's not true, don't let it come out of your mouth.

When something shaded, spun, or less than true does come out of your mouth, learn from it. Don't go down into a pit. Consider what you said and what you wish you had said (perhaps nothing!). Play the scenario out in your mind. Prepare for next time. Move on.

If you've lied to someone, make it right. Own up. Apologize sincerely, with no excuses. Be clear and straightforward.

Yes, this can be terrifying, but owning up is healthy. It's honesty in action.

Be real. Own up when you mess up. Your heart loves this. More honesty will be the result.

Honest doesn't just happen. You must practice it. As you do, you'll be amazed at the results, both for you and for those around you.

As you live more honestly from your heart, the more you'll care about the welfare of others and less about what they say and do. You'll care more about serving than about how others respond. You'll live more in line with your mission and be less influenced by the negative stuff swirling around you.

In other words, you'll be freer to be who you really are. You'll be authentic. You'll be honest. Your difference-making power will multiply.

MISSION BUILDER #7: PATIENCE (THE ABILITY TO WAIT)

We Google almost everything. We get hundreds of thousands of results in a fraction of a second. We're used to quick and fast. Instant everything.

If we have to wait, even a little bit, we grow antsy. Then we get frustrated — and even angry.

We don't like waiting. It's a nuisance.

No wonder our anxiety and depression rates have skyrocketed. We want what we want, and we want it now — including fixes, feel goods, success, wealth, popularity, and anything else we might desire. If we don't understand the first time around, we walk away. If we try something and don't get it right away, then it's not for us.

Think how much we're missing out on by not waiting.

Every substantially good thing I can think of in life takes time. Some of them a *lot* of time.

Exposing the lies you've swallowed and lived is a process that takes time.

Learning truths to replace those lies is a process that takes time.

Learning to love other people well isn't quick or instantaneous. You'll be learning that on a deeper level your entire life.

Difference-making is the journey of a lifetime and the road goes on and on. Time is required.

Difference Makers develop the ability to wait. They learn to be patient with themselves, others, and the world at large.

Patience — the willingness to wait — is a powerful weapon in the Difference Maker's arsenal. Haste often leads to poor decisions, frustration, and then rework. Tough choices become clear with time. The heart needs time to filter through things and come to the truth.

Difference Makers learn to embrace patience. Waiting is a key life skill.

MISSION BUILDER #8: PERSEVERANCE / ENDURANCE

Difference-making requires guts. You have to get out of your comfort zone and then stick with it.

Good things take time. Developing new patterns is a process. Learning to use the new tools in your mission toolbox requires perseverance.

Keep in mind that you're not just learning life skills, but you're practicing and honing them over time. There will be ups and downs. Successes and failures. Good days and not so good ones. It's a bit of a roller coaster.

And what do you do on roller coasters?

Keep your arms and legs inside. Keep the security bar firmly fastened in place. Hang on. Have as much fun as possible. Scream when necessary — or when you just want to.

Most roller coasters are over in about 90 seconds. Life goes on a bit longer than that. It can be exhausting, draining, and challenging. Perseverance and endurance are required.

Difference-making is not an overnight event. It's not something you can check off a list. It's a lifestyle that's developed over days, weeks, months, and years.

Difference-making is like a big boulder on top of a mountain. It takes a lot of energy to get it moving, but once it does, it's all downhill from there. Difference-making picks up speed and power over time.

Be persevering now and watch what happens down the road. Stick with it. Endure. The results can be astounding.

MISSION BUILDER #9: KINDNESS / COMPASSION

Personally, I think it's easier to be kind than mean.

> *A genuine smile can have a huge impact.*
> *A kind word can lift the heart.*
> *A kind gesture can calm fear.*
> *A kind act can lighten a burden.*
> *A kind lifestyle can become a magnet.*
> *Kindness is contagious.*
> *Difference Makers are kind.*

Why be mean? Why be surly and angry? Why not be decent and warm to those around us? Simple respect is a great kindness that is becoming rarer by the day.

If you observe and listen, you'll be genuinely interested. If you're genuinely interested, you'll be willing to wait and even persevere to love and support someone else. This adds up to kindness.

Once kindness has a hold on a heart, it rarely lets go. Kindness is intoxicating. Kindness meets deep needs in others that we're not aware of.

You don't need to know their secrets. You don't have to be aware of their challenges. You can choose to be kind, period.

When you are kind, difference-making is automatic.

MISSION BUILDER #10: FORGIVENESS

Life is full of wounds. We receive them, and we give them. How we deal with them matters deeply.

The basic meaning of forgiveness is *to release*. When you forgive someone, you're releasing them. You're also releasing your own heart to not be controlled by them or what they said or did.

Forgiveness is medicine for wounded hearts. It frees them to heal rather than become dark, bitter, or vengeful.

Forgiveness of ourselves releases us to continue. When we fall, we get up quickly. We own up. We ask forgiveness, if appropriate. We forgive and release ourselves.

Difference Makers hold offenses and wounds lightly. They learn to cling to kindness, hope, and love instead. They refuse to be bogged down with what happened and who did what. They can't afford such weights. The world needs them.

Difference Makers get good at forgiveness. Their hearts travel as light as possible.

FILLING YOUR MISSION TOOLBOX WITH MISSION BUILDERS

Mission Busters aren't worth your time. They are life-suckers. Life is hard enough without those leeches.

Instead, intentionally fill your life toolbox with Mission Builders.

Observe. See people and the world around you. Get out of your own head and pay attention.

Pursue humility. Right-size yourself. You are valuable, unique, and imperfect. You are a Difference Maker, but you are not God.

Learn to *accept yourself* for who you are and where you are. As you do, you can move on and grow, step by step.

Listen. Try to hear the heart behind their words.

As you observe and listen, you'll find yourself being *genuinely interested*. People will sense this and respond.

If you're willing to wait, you'll find yourself developing *patience and perseverance*. You'll make wiser decisions and fewer mistakes. You'll have more impact in the lives of others.

Be kind. Your heart loves this. So do other people. When kindness is present, everyone wins.

Learn to forgive others and yourself quickly. Wounds will come. You will mess up. Release others and yourself quickly. Refuse to get caught in guilt and shame.

CONSIDER:

Just putting tools in your mission toolbox isn't enough. You need to use them.

Let's consider our mission builder list again:

Observation
Humility
Self-acceptance
Listening
Genuine interest in others
Patience
Perseverance and endurance
Kindness
Forgiveness

Which one of these Mission Builders is strongest in your life? Which one do you think is the weakest?

Now, rank these mission builders, from 1 to 10, with 1 being the strongest and 10 being the weakest in your life.

Make your own list of these Mission Builders and the Mission Busters. Copy it. Place it in strategic places where you will see it throughout your day.

Make a plan to read this list at least once a day. I recommend reading it once in the morning near the start of your day, and then once in the evening as a sort of review.

Let this list of Mission Busters and Mission Builders sink into your mind and heart. Be aware of the Busters and focus on the Builders.

If you want to go a step further, in addition to reading the list daily, pick a Mission Builder for the day to be more aware of and to work on.

"Today, I will work on observing."
"Today, I'll set my mind to be kind."
"Today, I'll not make things about me, but listen to those around me."

Yes, you'll fail from time to time. When you do, forgive yourself quickly. Move on. Get up and move forward. Don't let guilt and shame take hold.

Remember, you're learning. You're not going to get this perfectly. Let it be enough to learn and grow in these things over time. Put in the effort and you will see results.

Difference Makers are aware of Mission Busters but focus on Mission Builders. They look ahead and move forward, one day, one step at a time.

CHAPTER 27
MISSION LAUNCH!

IN THE LAST SEVERAL CHAPTERS, we've talked about defining your mission. No matter what your mission is, it must flow from your heart. It will be about people, love, and service. We talked about Mission Busters and Mission Builders. You need to be aware of the Mission Busters, but don't focus there. Pour your energies into Mission Builders. Fill your mission toolbox with effective, powerful tools that will help get you far down the road of difference-making.

In this chapter, we're honing in on actually writing your mission. Once you finalize it, we'll talk about how to begin living it — today.

WRITING YOUR MISSION.

Simple is better.

Life is complicated. People can be complex. Your mission doesn't have to be.

In fact, in terms of writing your mission, the simpler the better. Let's take a crack at it.

Here are the four key words to your mission that we talked about earlier:

Heart

Your mission must flow from your heart. The words you choose to express your mission need to resonate deeply with you.

People

Life is about relationships. Your mission will include people. This needs to be expressed somehow.

Love

Your mission isn't about convenience or comfort. It's about extending yourself for others. It's about thinking, speaking, and acting for the good of those around you. It needs to be clear that your mission is about love.

Service

Service and love are two sides of the same coin. Genuine service is love-motivated. Your mission needs to state that you're in this thing to make a positive difference.

Heart. People. Love. Service.

Here are some examples.

> *"My mission is to live from my heart for others."*
> *"Genuine me, in genuine love, in genuine service to others."*
> *"My heart, for people, in love and service."*
> *"I'm here to love and serve from the heart."*
> *"My heart, my life, for others, for good."*
> *"Here to love and serve."*

You get the idea.

Your turn.

Play with it a little. Brainstorm. Write down several, even many possibilities.

Remember, keep it simple. It doesn't have to be a sentence. A phrase will do.

MISSION POSSIBILITIES:

_____
_____
_____
_____
_____
_____
_____
_____
_____

Now, which one grabs you the most?

For now, this is it.

Write it down. Several times. Post it where you can see it several times a day. Let your new mission statement work on you.

After several days, ask yourself how you're feeling about it. Do you want to adjust it at all?

Remember, don't complicate it. Keep it simple, short, to the point.

> *Your mission doesn't need to say everything.*
> *It is a short, direct phrase or sentence that describes*
> *the big idea of what you're about.*
> *It describes who and how you want to be. It*
> *describes who and how you <u>will</u> be.*
> *It says, "Difference Maker here!"*

Look at your mission phrase often. Ponder it. Let it soak into your mind and heart.

> *Difference Makers discover their mission, state it simply, and let it sink deeply into their hearts.*

CHAPTER 28
WHERE DO YOU GO FROM HERE?

Give a person a big enough <u>why</u> and they can endure any <u>what</u>.

YOU NEED A *WHY*.
You need a big *why*. A massive *why*.
How do you discover your *why*?
You're almost there. Your *why* is the driving force behind your mission.

Why are you here?

To make a difference.
You're here for impact.
You're here to contribute good and healing to a broken and hurting world.
You're a wounded healer.
You're here to make a difference.
How much of a difference can you make? More than you could ever dream possible. Who knows who you could become?
It's not about money. It's not about fame. It's not about accumulating stuff, moving up, or succeeding according to the world's definition.

It's about people. It's about love and service. It's about your heart.

As you embrace your identity as a Difference Maker and live like one, others will notice. You'll become contagious, in a good way. People will be drawn to you. They will watch you, be inspired, and then begin to make a difference themselves.

They too were designed for relationship and impact. When they see this in you, their hearts come alive. They want more. They follow. They learn. They begin to break out of where they are and set out on their Difference Maker journey.

The ripple effect of difference-making is actually less like a ripple — which slowly weakens as it progresses — and more like a building tsunami that gains power and momentum with each positive thought, word, and action.

So, grab onto your <u>why</u>.

WHAT'S YOUR WHY?

You're a Difference Maker. You're here to make a difference. You're designed for impact.

> *When life gets tough, and it will, come back to your why.*
> *When people don't respond well, and you feel rejected, remember your why.*
> *When you make a mistake or fail, breathe deeply, get up, and remember your why.*
> *When bad things happen that are beyond your control, focus on your why.*

No matter what happens to or around you, you are here to love and serve. This is the only kind of life that will bring fulfillment, contentment, and true joy.

You're a Difference Maker. When you don't live out who you are, you grow frustrated, confused, angry, and even bitter. A non-difference-making life is an empty one.

The Difference Maker journey is hard and challenging at times precisely because it is good. The best things in life involve getting out of our comfort zones and stretching ourselves.

Difference-making is costly. You must be committed.

And yes, it's worth it.

It's worth it for your family and friends.

It's worth it for the world around you.

It's worth it for you — your own mental, physical, emotional, and spiritual health.

You're on the Difference Maker road. Stay on it. If you find yourself wandering, come back to this book. Remind yourself of your *why*. Set your mind firmly on difference-making and living out your mission.

You will live out who you really believe yourself to be.

You are a Difference Maker.
Accept it. Embrace it. Live it.

SET A FEW GOALS

You know your mission. Write it down again.

Again, it should be short, simple, and to the point. Remember the four keys: Heart, People, Love, and Service.

MY MISSION:

_____

Read your mission out loud.

Read it again, slowly. Let it sink in.

Now, ask yourself the question, *"How can I live this out in the near future?"*

Start small. Come up with one goal you would like work on this week. Pick something that's definitely doable, but that also stretches you.

If it's a totally comfortable goal, it's too easy. We grow when we stretch.

Again, the goal needs to be doable, but also stretching. Write it down.

MY GOAL THIS WEEK:

_____

_____

_____

Here are some examples.

Sample mission: "See. Listen. Serve."
Possible goals:
I will work on being quiet and seeing the people around me. I'll review how I did at the end of each day.

When people talk to me, I'll stop thinking about my response and focus on them, their eyes, their words, and their heart.

At night with my family, I'll focus on asking good questions and listening well. I'll set my mind to do this on the way home from work.

Sample mission: "Live large by serving others."
Possible goals:
This week I'll engage with those the behind-the-scenes people who serve me (janitors, construction workers, cashiers, food service workers, etc.), call them by name (if I can), and tell them thank you.

I'll think of 3 people in my life who inspire and motivate me. I'll tell them they inspire me, thank them, and share my mission with them.

I'll think of someone I know who needs encouragement. I'll contact them and be ready to listen.

When the week is done, evaluate how you did.
Celebrate any progress you made.

If you feel like you've failed, don't worry about it. Release yourself from guilt. Remember that guilt is not your friend. It keeps you stuck. Keep taking action.

Set a goal for the next week. When that week is done, evaluate, and set a goal for the next week. And so on.

When you live out who you are as a Difference Maker, your heart will grow. You'll find yourself more inspired and motivated. Difference-making is a snowball rolling downhill. It might take some effort to get started, but once you're rolling, your new difference-making habits will pick up speed and momentum.

Set a time, once a week, for goal setting and review.
It shouldn't take much time. Only a few minutes, most likely. Put it on your schedule. Set an alarm on your phone. Stick to it.

As you set and review goals from week to week, you'll find yourself growing more confident.

Again, make sure the goal is doable, but that it also stretches you.

To help out, you can download a simple Goal Setting and Review sheet at https://www.garyroe.com/difference-maker-goal-setting
In this download, you'll also get some hints and guidance for setting some bigger goals down the road.

LIVE YOUR MISSION!

Knowing your mission is a wonderful start. Putting some feet to your mission and living it out is exciting, motivating, and contagious.

You're a Difference Maker.

Know it. Embrace it. Live it.

Difference Makers cling to their mission, set goals that stretch them, and regularly evaluate and adjust.

CHAPTER 29
PUTTING IT ALL TOGETHER

WELL, DIFFERENCE MAKER, YOU'VE DONE it. You're almost done with the book.

Your Difference Maker journey, on the other hand, is just beginning.

> *The world needs you.*
> *You can do this.*
> *This is a battle.*
> *Be aware of the lies.*
> *Focus on the truths.*
> *Learn to handle the obstacles, and then hurdle them.*

Some obstacles will boomerang back, again and again. No problem. Handle them again, and then hurdle them, again.

Know your mission.

Grab it with both hands. Hold on tight. Set your mind on it.

Say it in the morning when you wake up. Speak it out loud again at night when you go to bed.

Set simple, weekly goals. Make sure they're doable, but that they also stretch you.

Thank you for being willing to go on this Difference Maker journey. You'll be challenged. Not everyone will respond well to the new, difference-making you. Some people will try to distract you.

Others will attempt to rattle you and hold you back. The world will try to derail you and get you off track.

Don't let them.

Stand firm. Stay the course.

You know who you are. You know what you're about. Keep your *why* in sight.

You're going to need help in this journey. The people around you will make all the difference.

Get around other Difference Makers.

Expose your heart to people who inspire and motivate you. You will become like the people you are around the most. Choose your associations wisely.

Gear up for battle.
And have some fun.

There's nothing, I mean nothing, like living from your heart in love and service to others.

Now go. Become the Difference Maker you were designed to be.

Difference Makers know why they're here.
They discover their mission and live it with passion.
They know everything flows from their hearts.
Their mission is about people, love, and service.
We will discover our why.
We will live our mission.
We will live from our hearts.
We will love and serve for the greater good.
We are Difference Makers.

Please make sure you get your free, exclusive download:
Difference-Maker Summary and Goal Setting Sheets
https://www.garyroe.com/difference-maker-goal-setting

CHAPTER 30
MY AMAZING DIFFERENCE-MAKING MENTOR

THANK YOU FOR TAKING YOUR heart seriously and reading this book. I hope you found it engaging, challenging, and inspiring. You are a Difference Maker. Never forget that.

I can't close this book, however, without giving credit to the ultimate Difference Maker in my life.

IMPERFECT PEOPLE NEED GOOD MENTORS.

If you're perfect, you don't need a mentor. But since one of our basic truths is that we're all imperfect, we all need help. We need models. We need examples. We need other Difference Makers.

I'm a Difference Maker, but I don't have it all together. Far from it. Like you, I'm human, and that comes with a large set of limitations and vulnerabilities. I battle daily with issues stemming from past trauma and hits that I've endured. I stumble a lot in life.

I do my best to get up, dust myself off, and find a way to grow and make a difference. I'm focused on learning from the messes I create. There is no time to wallow in self-pity or guilt. Time is moving, and I have a limited amount of it on this earth. It's not what I did, but what I do next that matters most now.

The Difference Maker I am and have become is due to those who have gone before me. As I've said before, I stand on the shoulders of others. Particularly, there's one set of shoulders that has supported me like no other. He is the ultimate Difference Maker in my life.

He is my continual mentor. I'm honored to be able to call him my friend. His name is Jesus Christ.

If you come from a different faith or perhaps claim no faith at all, I'm not out to cause you distress. My purpose is to encourage and challenge you.

My basic message is this. You need an ultimate difference-making mentor in your life — one that is head and shoulders above all the others. One who will be committed to you personally and walk with you through your failures and successes.

Choose that mentor carefully. Your difference-making impact depends on it.

MENTORING HAPPENS OVER TIME.

How did I choose my ultimate difference-making mentor?

It happened over time. Pain and need drove me to him.

You've heard parts of my story in chapter two. I want to go back and emphasize a few things here.

As a kid, sexual abuse, loss, and death assaulted my heart. My innocence was violently stolen, and along with it my sense of safety and security. I lost relatives, friends, pets, and parents. The world became a confusing, unfriendly, and dangerous place.

Novelist Natsume Soseki said, *"In the midst of a world that moves, I alone am still."* That described me. I felt different, damaged, and out-of-place. As a child and a teen, I felt isolated, sad, and lonely most of the time.

Deep inside, I had this persistent, nagging feeling that I was bad. I didn't deserve to be here. The lies that formed over the years had sunk deep into my psyche. I felt like I didn't belong.

My life as I had known it certainly died with Dad. Mom didn't want to parent and probably couldn't. I didn't dare look ahead. I was terrified about what might be next.

I went through the motions. I went to school. I swam. I did

well at both, but inside, where no one else could see, my resolve was weakening. I could feel myself slipping away, day by day.

I went home each day to an empty apartment. Mom was undergoing inpatient psychiatric care after a suicide attempt. I would turn on all the lights and crank up the music. Maybe light and noise could keep the darkness at bay.

Then one day, out of nowhere, there was a knock on my apartment door.

I opened the door to find my best friend and his dad standing there. "Gary, we want you to come live with us," they said. I stood there, stunned. I stammered something about needing my mom's permission.

After Mom's discharge, I gathered my belongings and we drove over to my friend's house. Mom's terse farewell and abrupt departure left me feeling ashamed and embarrassed.

I stepped over the threshold. That moment was the beginning. I had no idea, but my entire life had made an abrupt, infinitesimally positive turn. I couldn't sense it yet, but I had walked through the door of what had to be one of the safest families on the planet.

Even though they already had four kids, they loved, accepted, and supported me in every way imaginable. Some days I wondered if this could be real. It was so good, in fact, that I simply couldn't take it all in.

After about six months adjusting to all this goodness, I knocked on the dad's office door.

"Can I ask you a question?" I said awkwardly.

He looked up from his desk. "Of course, Gary. Sit down."

As I lowered myself into the chair, I found myself asking, "Why in the world would you take in a kid like me?"

He blinked, then smiled. Leaning forward, he replied, "Gary, with what Jesus Christ did for us, how could we not do this for you?"

We were both quiet for a moment.

Then he leaned back and said, "He makes all the difference. If you let him, he will make all the difference for you."

"Thank you, sir," I said. We stood up together. He reached across the desk and shook my hand.

"It's an honor to know you, Gary," he said.

I looked into his eyes. He meant it.

To make a detailed, somewhat complicated, and long story short, Jesus became my mentor that day. He took me on, and I accepted his leadership.

His patience with me has been nothing short of astounding. His kind instruction and guidance has been truly remarkable. His unwavering commitment to me through more pain, loss, and difficulty has kept me sane. His unconditional acceptance of me through failure, doubt, and uncertainty has empowered me to rise from the dirt time and time again. His constant inspiration and encouragement have kept me leaning forward.

For me, Jesus is the ultimate Difference Maker.

He is my mentor. He has become my life. He is my *why*.

A LIFE OF OVERCOMING

I close with something Jesus said that has made a profound impact on me. I ponder these words almost daily.

"I have said these things to you so that in me you may have peace. In this world, you will have trouble. Take heart, for I have overcome the world." (John 16:33)

Difference-making is an ongoing battle. I expect to get shot at in life. I rise in the morning and know that obstacles await. Trouble abounds.

I need a mentor whose leadership can give me peace. I need someone who can overcome every obstacle that can be thrown at me. According to Jesus, he can, and already has.

You need a mentor like this. We all do.

Choose your ultimate difference-making mentor well.

The world is waiting.

RESOURCES FOR DIFFERENCE MAKERS

Resources to help you heal and grow from the losses of life, so that you can be more of the Difference Maker you were made to be.

Comfort for Grieving Hearts: Hope and Encouragement for Times of Loss

We all need comfort. We long for it. Written as a companion for you on your grief journey, this book reads as a warm conversation between the author and someone who's grieving. Chapters are brief, easy-to-read, and practical, giving you bite-sized bits of comfort, encouragement, and healing over time. *Comfort for Grieving Hearts* is a USA Best Book Awards Winner. For more information or to download a free excerpt, visit www.garyroe.com.

Teen Grief: Caring for the Grieving Teenage Heart

Teens are hurting. We can't afford to allow pain and loss to get the better of them. Written at the request of parents, teachers, coaches, and school counselors, *Teen Grief* is informative, practical, and full of guidance, insight, and ideas for assisting teens navigate the turbulent waters of loss. *Teen Grief* is a Book Excellence Award Winner and has received rave reviews from those who live and work with teens. For more information or to download a free excerpt, visit www.garyroe.com.

Shattered: Surviving the Loss of a Child

The loss of a child is a terrible thing. Written at the request of grieving parents and grandparents, *Shattered* has been called "one of the most comprehensive and practical grief books available." The book combines personal stories, compassionate guidance, and practical suggestions designed to help shattered hearts navigate this devastating loss. A Best Book Awards Finalist, *Shattered* has received sterling reviews by both mental health professionals and grieving parents. For more information or to download a free excerpt, visit www.garyroe.com.

Please Be Patient, I'm Grieving: How to Care for and Support the Grieving Heart

People often feel misunderstood, judged, and even rejected during a time of loss. Gary wrote this book by request to help others better understand and support grieving hearts and to help grieving hearts understand themselves. A group discussion guide is included. *Please Be Patient, I'm Grieving* is a Best Book Awards Finalist. For more information or to download a free excerpt, visit www.garyroe.com.

Heartbroken: Healing from the Loss of a Spouse

Losing a spouse is painful, confusing, and often traumatic. This comforting and practical book was penned from the stories of dozens of widows and widowers. Its simple, straightforward approach has emotionally impacted hearts and helped thousands know they're not alone, not crazy, and that they will make it. *Heartbroken* is a Best Book Award Finalist and a National Indie Excellence Book Award Finalist. For more information or to download a free excerpt, visit www.garyroe.com.

Saying Goodbye: Facing the Loss of a Loved One

Full of stories, this warm, easy-to-read, and beautifully illustrated gift book has comforted thousands. It reads like a conversation with a close friend giving wise counsel and hope to those facing a loss. Co-authored with New York Times' Bestseller Cecil Murphey, this attractive hardback edition is available at www.garyroe.com.

FREE ON GARY'S WEBSITE

The Good Grief Mini-Course
Full of personal stories, inspirational content, and practical assignments, this 8-session email series is designed to help readers understand grief and deal with its roller-coaster emotions. Thousands have been through **Good Grief**, which is now being used in support groups as well. Available at www.garyroe.com.

The Hole in my Heart: Tackling Grief's Tough Questions
This easy-to-read ebook tackles some of grief's big questions: "How did this happen?" "Why?" "Am I crazy?" "Am I normal?" "Will this get any easier?" plus others. Written in the first person, **The Hole in My Heart** engages and comforts the heart. Available at www.garyroe.com.

I Miss You: A Holiday Survival Kit
Thousands have downloaded this brief, easy-to-read ebook. **I Miss You** provides some basic, simple tools on how to use holidays and special times to grieve well and love those around you. Available at https://www.garyroe.com.

ABOUT THE AUTHOR

Gary's story began with a childhood of mixed messages and sexual abuse. This was followed by other losses and numerous grief experiences.

Ultimately, a painful past led Gary into a life of helping wounded people heal and grow. He says, "My goal is to inspire and challenge myself and others to overcome adversity, turn pain into purpose, and be the Difference Makers we were designed to be." A former college minister, missionary in Japan, entrepreneur in Hawaii, and pastor in Texas and Washington, he now serves as a writer, speaker, hospice chaplain, and grief counselor.

Gary is the multiple award-winning author of numerous books, including the bestsellers *Comfort for Grieving Hearts, Shattered: Surviving the Loss of a Child*, and *Please Be Patient, I'm Grieving*. He has been featured on Focus on the Family, CBN, Dr. Laura, Wellness.com, Thrive Global, Belief Net, and other major media.

He has more than 600 articles to his credit. Gary is the winner of the Diane Duncam Award for Excellence in Hospice Care and is a popular keynote and seminar speaker at a wide variety of venues.

Gary loves being a husband and father. He says, "I'm married to an amazing woman named Jen. She's my hero. She's been through more than you can imagine and has come out on the other side. She's a Difference Maker, and she makes my life better each day. I have seven adopted kids. They're an amazing crew. They keep me laughing, scratching my head, and growing. I have two grandkids, so far. Life is busy."

Gary enjoys swimming, hockey, corny jokes, and cool Hawaiian shirts. Gary and his family live in Texas. Visit him at www.garyroe.com and follow him on Facebook, Twitter, LinkedIn, and Pinterest.

Links: Facebook: https://www.facebook.com/garyroeauthor
Twitter: https://twitter.com/GaryRoeAuthor
LinkedIn: https://www.linkedin.com/in/garyroeauthor
Pinterest: https://www.pinterest.com/garyroe79/

AN URGENT REQUEST

(Can You Help Me Out?)

One last thing...

If you found this book helpful and inspiring, I need your help.

Could you help me reach others with the Difference Maker message?

You can be a Difference Maker by writing a simple review of this book and posting it on whatever site you purchased it from.

Just answer this question.

How did this book affect you?

Make it short and sweet, 1-3 sentences.

I read these reviews. They help me be a better writer and become even more of the Difference Maker I was designed to be.

Your review helps us reach more people. It may seem like a small thing, but it has great impact.

Thanks for your help!

www.ingramcontent.com/pod-product-compliance
Lightning Source LLC
Chambersburg PA
CBHW030053100526
44591CB00008B/135